the ART
and SCIENCE
of Happiness

10 SIMPLE STEPS to learn how to
ENJOY LIFE AGAIN

by Ira Vouk

Nov 30, 2022
San Diego, CA
Cover photo by Lana & Igor Dovbenko
ISBN: 978-1-387-46900-0

There is nothing either good or bad, but thinking makes it so.

"Hamlet" by William Shakespeare

"We are currently in a considerable happiness drought in modern day society, and that's why this book is so important! It does an admirable job of tackling personal happiness; what it is, and the steps to implement to achieve it. This is a book I will refer to repeatedly because at the very least, these types of reminders will put us back on track. A helpful and easy read that anyone can learn from."

Nick Trenton,
Acclaimed author of 20+ books including the #1 Amazon Bestseller 'Stop Overthinking'

છ

"In this highly readable and enjoyable book, Ira Vouk tells us that happiness is a skill one can learn—it is not derived from a magical pill we can take or from having lots of money, nice cars, real estate, or even the perfect body. She then provides, using simple and accessible language, a list of ten concepts and tools that, if used consistently, will lead to greater happiness. These include such things as practicing self-acceptance, gratitude, meditation, and helping others. Best of all, recommendations, along with practice activities in this book are not based solely upon the author's impressions; rather they are based upon theory and research in the burgeoning field of positive psychology. With the inclusion of practice activities that are research-based, The Art and Science of Happiness is a valuable addition to anyone's library and demonstrates that happiness is achievable by all of us."

Donna Castañeda,
Ph.D., Professor, San Diego State University, Department of Psychology

"Based on over 25 years of working with individuals, couples and families, what brings people to therapy is a desire to be happier in their lives. Whether the symptoms are depressive or anxious or their connections to others are dissatisfying, the outcome they are seeking is happiness. There are many books that describe a construct for happiness but so many of them ultimately discourage the reader. In this book, Ira presents the latest science combined with the tools the reader needs, to implement a system to obtain and maintain a higher happiness baseline. And that can be life altering. She has the courage to present cutting edge use of alternatives to traditional pharmaceuticals such as psychedelics, in an easy to read and understand book that leaves the reader encouraged to follow the plan."

Daniel Kane,
ED.S, MA, LMHC, Licensed Mental Health Professional and Practicing Psychotherapist

&

"Reading about how to recalibrate my emotional baseline was very valuable and timely. This book is very easy to read. It presents a lot of options for people to follow as they try to make improvements to their emotional wellbeing. If they are smart, they will follow all of the exercises but I can see how just a few of them can go a long way to making positive changes."

Jeiselle London,
Writer

&

"A very enjoyable and enlightening book that is easy to read. Vouk does her research and, through this, helps you realize that anyone can achieve happiness. This book is a good reminder that we are in charge of our feelings more than we know."

Cobey Mandarino,
Executive Coach

Foreword

And there I was... shattered, broken, dead inside. I woke up before the alarm went off (again), with no desire to open my eyes and get up, with no desire to live. I had lost count of how many days (weeks, months??) went by like that. I was an empty shell of a human, having to function just because I had kids to take care of. They needed to go to school, they needed to eat, they needed a mother. That was the only thing keeping me alive. Or, rather, at least visibly alive.

Life is a weird and unpredictable thing. And sometimes shit hits the fan and you find yourself in unbearable pain. I'm not talking about physical pain, we all know how to deal with that. I'm talking about the illness of the soul that, if not healed, results in a depression, in some cases – suicide. It happens to many, throughout our lives.

That pain that follows you wherever you go, when you wake up miserable, fall asleep miserable, when you cry when no one is watching. It becomes part of you, to the point when you start forgetting what it feels like – to live without constantly hurting. Sometimes you may even have psychosomatic experiences like real chest pain or difficulty breathing – real body aches resulting from a psychological trauma.

Maybe some of you are experiencing this right now. If so – be strong. There's a way out, I promise. I hope this book helps you find yourself so that you can resurrect. If it helps at least 1 person – that's all that matters to me.

Or maybe you're one of those people who just forgot how to smile because you've buried yourself in responsibilities, chores and duties. Because you have a job that you don't like. Because you're married to the wrong person. Because your parents don't appreciate you. Because... the list goes on. Because you're living somebody else's life and not your own.

For a number of years, I didn't know what a natural, sincere smile felt like. I forgot what happiness felt like. I was depressed. I started searching for ways to learn how to be happy again. And I found them. So I want to share them with you.

I believe I can help a lot of people learn how to be happy again because there are specific, scientifically proven things that anyone can do – simple things that work.

Fast forward a couple years from the day when I realized I was almost dead...

Today I am a person who is thankful for every single day of her life, who wakes up with a smile every morning and goes to bed with a smile every night, a loving mother who enjoys spending time with her precious children, a professional with multiple published best-seller books, an educator, and a businesswoman. Every single day I only do things I want to do. I never do anything because I have to. I radiate love and I'm capable of truly loving others because I have a lot to give. I truly enjoy life and I consider myself an eternally happy individual. I'm happier than I have ever been, and it's not because I won a lottery...

It's because I have taught myself the skill of happiness. And you can do that, too. It's actually pretty easy. I wrote this book for YOU in the hope that you will take full advantage of this knowledge and turn your life in the direction of complete contentment and joy that you can also share with others.

I've been studying this topic for a long time. I have gathered and digested vast amounts of information and have practiced many things. In this book, I will describe the mechanism of happiness that truly works. Hope this helps those who need it.

Hugs.

Ira Vouk

Contents

Introduction

"Our intentional, effortful activities have a powerful effect on how happy we are, over and above the effects of our set points and the circumstances in which we find ourselves."
Sonja Lyubomirsky, professor of Psychology, UCR

The sad truth

As I was doing my research on happiness in an attempt to find a way to resurrect myself, I discovered I wasn't alone... mildly speaking. Turns out, there are millions of people who forgot how to smile. Moreover, these days it seems more of a norm to be sad than to be happy. This is despite the fact that most of us, at least in the US, finally have all our basic physical needs met, and more.

"Compared with their grandparents, today's young adults have grown up with much more affluence, slightly less happiness and much greater risk of depression and assorted social pathology..." [1] says David Myers, the author of "The American Paradox: Spiritual Hunger in an Age of Plenty".

The observation that economic growth does not necessarily go together with increasing life satisfaction was first made over 50 years ago. Since then, there has been much discussion over what came to be known as the 'Easterlin Paradox'. At the heart of the paradox was the fact that in some countries happiness was not increasing with rising national incomes. [2] "Our becoming much

---

[1] David Myers, "The American Paradox: Spiritual Hunger in an Age of Plenty" (2000)

[2] Our World In Data: Happiness and Life Satisfaction (May 2017): https://ourworldindata.org/happiness-and-life-satisfaction

better off over the last decades has not been accompanied by one iota of increased subjective well-being." (David Myers)

I'll provide some facts to support the above, because I'm a nerd and I believe in data more than I believe in subjective opinions.

Illnesses of the mind-brain affect tens of millions of people in the United States. Depression is by far the most prevalent, representing 99 percent of all mind-brain illnesses.[3] It is associated with symptoms such as melancholy, loss of pleasure, loss of energy, difficulty in concentrating, and suicidal thoughts.

Depression in the US affects over 18 million (!!!) adults in any given year. It is the leading cause of disability for ages 15-44.[4]

... It is also the primary reason why someone dies of suicide about every 12 minutes – over 41,000 people a year.[5]

Now, I'm sure all of us remember 2020 and what followed. Uncertainty, lockdowns, panic on social media, closures of businesses, overflowing hospitals, deaths of family members, the list goes on. Would you think that could have affected our mental state? No kidding. It certainly didn't help us feel happier. We weren't a cheerful nation to start with, but now things are even worse for many.

---

[3] American Psychiatric Association. Diagnostic and Statistical Manual of Mental Disorders, fourth edition, text revision, DSM-!V – TR. Washington, DC 2000.

[4] Hope for Depression Research Foundation: Depression Facts: https://www.hopefordepression.org/depression-facts/

[5] Centers for Disease Control and Prevention (CDC) Web -based Injury Statistics Query and Reporting System (WISQARS): http://www.cdc.gov/injury/wisqars/index.html

The Substance Abuse and Mental Health Services Administration recently provided shocking stats on the amount of people who experienced symptoms of depression or suicidal thoughts as a result of the pandemic, as well as increased alcohol and drug use.[6]

Now, here's a list of countries with the highest depression rates as of 2022.[7] Note, the only country that is ahead of us is the one that has recently become an active war zone! Isn't this sad??

1. Ukraine (their happiness levels were higher before 2022)
2. United States (plus, what about the ones who are unhappy but refuse to admit that? I bet if we record those – we can beat Ukraine)
3. Estonia
4. Australia
5. Brazil
6. Greece
7. Portugal
8. Belarus (my home country; no comments on this one, I don't want to go to jail)
9. Finland
10. Lithuania

Least depressed countries (God bless them):

1. Solomon Islands
2. Papua New Guinea
3. Timor - Leste

---

[6] Substance Abuse and Mental Health Services Administration: 2020 NSDUH Detailed Tables: https://www.samhsa.gov/data/sites/default/files/reports/rpt35323/NSDUHDetailedTabs2020/NSDUHDetailedTabs2020/NSDUHDetailedTabsTOC2020.htm#toc

[7] World Health Organization: Depression and Other Common Mental Disorders (2022): https://www.who.int/publications/i/item/depression-global-health-estimates

4. Vanuatu
5. Kiribati
6. Tonga

Moral of the story: Americans, don't go to Solomon Islands, don't mess with those wonderful happy people who still remember why they were born.

Clearly now more than ever, we as a nation, need to remember how to smile… **And we have an option to either allow our misery and sadness to control us, be depressed for life, start taking Prozac or other substances (legal and not so much) and sink deeper and deeper into the black hole of depression. Or – learn to be happy and live a high-quality life full of joy and purpose.**

And this is why I decided to write this book – *to help you make that choice and to show you the way.*

Looking back at my life, I realize that I have a pretty fascinating story: from cleaning toilets to becoming a best-selling author.

But what's more important is not my professional achievements. I have gone a long way from being miserable to learning how to fully enjoy life, every day, regardless of the circumstances. And I'm ready to tell you my story and show you how you can do the same.

This is my third book. Writing a book is like having a baby. You go through the pain of publishing one, then time goes by and all you remember are the pleasant things that come after, you don't remember the hassle and the pains, so somehow you are willing to do it again.

So here I am, doing it again.

The sad truth

I would say that this book is more important to me than others (though I do love all my babies) because I truly believe it can touch the lives of many people and make a bigger difference in the world.

This book is the culmination of my transformational journey. And hopefully yours.

The mechanism of feeling happy

While working on resurrecting myself like a phoenix from the ashes (an experience that led me to share my knowledge with the world) I discovered that there is no mystery in the mechanism of feeling happy. It's all just chemistry in your brain.

There are certain, and relatively simple, things we can do to become happier. What's interesting though is that most of the goals we think will make us happy – actually don't, especially in the long term!

Here is a number of "false goals" that Laurie Santos lists in her *free* online course "The Science of Well-Being"[8] offered by Yale University on Coursera (please promise me you'll take that course after you finish reading this book, it will change your life):

- Good job
- Lots of money
- Awesome stuff
- "True love"
- The perfect body
- The perfect grades

For the most part, we're actually clueless about what we need to do in order to become happy. We think we know. We get what we think will make us happier – and we become miserable. Believe me, I know. One of the most depressing moments of my life was when I realized I had achieved everything society had convinced me I should have achieved in life: high income, a few pieces of real-estate in the finest city in the universe, children, a fancy car with a red stripe on it, professional recognition. I found myself surprised and puzzled. "I have everything a human could possibly need. Why

[8] Coursera: The Science of Well-Being by Laurie Santos (offered by Yale): https://www.coursera.org/learn/the-science-of-well-being

am I miserable?" It took a few years of research to figure out what I TRULY needed to feel alive again.

So if things that we thought would make us happy – actually don't, then what does?

It's simple things that are described further in this book. *But it takes practice.*

We can tell ourselves: "This is all in our heads, we can just start feeling happy if we want to, because we can control our head." But that's not entirely true.

We absolutely cannot tell ourselves what to think and how to feel. If I tell you "don't think about a pink elephant," – I guarantee with 100 percent certainty that every single one of you will not be able to get rid of an image of the darn pink elephant in your head (it looks cute though, right?). Moral of the story: you can't fully control your mind.

The good news though, is that we're not absolutely hopeless. You can actually train your brain to think and feel a certain way, the way you want it to feel. And that is possible thanks to, what scientists call, "neuroplasticity"[9] – an ability of your brain to rewire (and not just in young ages), to modify the connections between neurons gradually through daily practice, and teach it how to behave in a different manner.

For those interested in learning more about how your brain works in general, here's a very useful video podcast episode[10] (see link in the footnote) from my favorite neuroscientist Andrew

---

[9] Patrice Voss et al, "Dynamic Brains and the Changing Rules of Neuroplasticity: Implications for Learning and Recovery" (2017)

[10] Huberman Lab: How Your Brain Works and Changes (January, 2021): https://hubermanlab.com/how-your-nervous-system-works-and-changes/

The mechanism of feeling happy

Huberman, a Stanford professor who has been lately popularizing the science of the human brain among us mere mortals.

Neuroplasticity is something that has been studied by scientists for a long time. What it means in simple words: your brain is plastic, like Play-Doh essentially. **It's moldable.** Though it doesn't mean you can just tell yourself to be happy after reading one book (even this book) or talking to your therapist a couple times. It doesn't happen that way. **You actually have to train it.** You have to teach it over a period of time to learn this new skill, just like with sports. And I'll help you teach your brain to be happy using its neuroplastic qualities.

Long story short: **you can train your brain to think and feel anything you want it to think and feel.** It just takes some time and practice. Not even a lot of time actually. If you practice the simple tools outlined in this book and you're disciplined about it – you will start feeling the difference within just 21 days. Confirmed by science and by me personally.

Some of you may say: "Bullshit, I was born this way, my brain chemistry dictates my misery, there's nothing I can do about it".

Others may say: "The circumstances in my life won't allow me to feel happy, my life is miserable because of the events and people around me".

But really, deep down you know that you can change the circumstances and/or the way you feel about them. So what it probably means is that you're just not interested in becoming a happy person. In that case – this book is not for you. Give it to your spouse.

According to Sonja Lyubomirsky, a psychology professor at UCR and author of the book "The How of Happiness"[11], "genes and circumstances don't matter as much as we think". Based on her research (at this point, you're probably starting to understand that I wasn't lying when I said I was a nerd but please forgive me for these references because I truly believe in data and research and my goal is to make sure that the material in this book is supported by science and is not perceived as my personal opinion)... So, based on her research, here is the spread of different factors affecting our mental state:

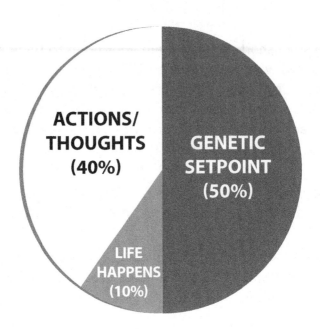

---

11 Sonja Lyubomirsky, "The How of Happiness: A New Approach to Getting the Life You Want" (2008)

So, reading between the lines:

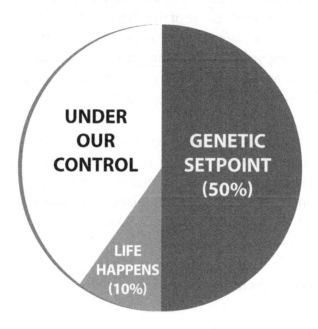

The thing is, positivity is something internal and it is not something that needs to be dependent on the circumstances. It's a state of mind. So instead of sitting, waiting for things to happen in your life that will magically make you happy, really all it takes is to **teach your brain how to be happy and change your life forever. It's not very difficult. And it works**. Because there are universal principles of how our brains and our minds work. It's the same as physical exercise. You go to the gym to build your muscles, or you practice to learn a new skill. In the same way, you can do exercises that will train your brain over some period of time to learn the skill of happiness. And it doesn't take long to take advantage of the neuroplasticity of your brain – typically about a month (or even less) is actually enough to see the change.

It's not the events in our lives that make us feel happy or unhappy. It's how we perceive them and react to them. So literally, it's all in our heads, it's not in our environment. And all our reactions have consequences. Because of this, "law of attraction" is not some mystical universal law of the universe – it's a logical consequence of your choices, your actions, what you say and how you perceive things. If you are generally happy and positive, you will make the choices to draw more of that into your life.

Moral of the story: even if you were born with a low natural level of dopamine (more on this can be found in the video podcast episode[12] referenced in the footnote), and if you feel like life circumstances, or people, are not fair to you – you absolutely can turn things around, take control of your own head and become happy again. Or not. It's your choice.

Yes. **YOUR choice.**

---

[12] Huberman Lan: Controlling Your Dopamine for Motivation, Focus and Satisfaction (September 2021): https://hubermanlab.com/controlling-your-dopamine-for-motivation-focus-and-satisfaction/

It's all about that base

And here's some background theory for better understanding.

It's all about the "baseline", or what some psychologists may call "a reference point". Let me explain.

There are things in everybody's lives that cause different emotions and cause us to feel either happy or unhappy when they happen. But what matters is your baseline state that doesn't depend on those events. If your baseline is one of a generally happy person, then you do much better with situations that will cause temporary unhappiness, or sadness, or anger, or any other emotions that people label as "negative". And there will always be ups and downs, it's impossible to be happy 24/7, 365 days of the year. Rather, what's important is to learn how to identify and register within your brain those moments of happiness, and then train your brain to feel them more and more often, thus elevating your baseline.

The problem with our generation (or, rather, with a few last generations) is that our "happiness baseline" is messed up.

We are born happy, perfect and whole.

But then we allow society to dictate its rules and put pressure on us and we convince ourselves that in order to be happy, to be whole and to be accepted, we need 1, 2, 3, etc (see picture #1). And you work your ass off your whole life to try to get 1, 2, 3 and maybe even 4, just so you can show everyone that you're cool and worthy. Meanwhile, you ignore the fact that you're miserable because that's not really what you wanted to do with your life. Been there, done that.

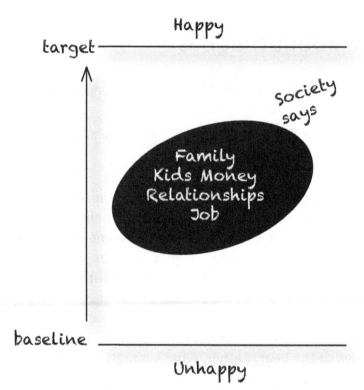

Happy

target

Society says

Family
Kids Money
Relationships
Job

baseline

Unhappy

For example, studies have shown that what we consider to be a "good income" and what we think our salary should be depends on what we know about other people's salaries. In our heads, it is not about how much money we really need to have a decent quality of life. For many, it's about keeping up with the Johnson's.

Social comparison is not a joke. It's a real problem in our society. Comparing makes us less happy. This is where social media is playing a very important role in our lives as well as TV commercials showcasing happy smiling people that possess products they're selling, making you want to be "like them". In 1997, a study[13] was published that showed that the more time you spend watching TV, the higher is your estimation of other people's wealth and, as a consequence, the lower is the estimation of your own wealth. Fast forward 3 decades: consumerism has reached the peak of

---

[13] Thomas C. O'Guinn et al, "The Role of Television in the Construction of Consumer Reality" (1997)

its evolution with the help of social media and targeted online advertising. As a result, we keep pushing ourselves further into the black hole of competitive misery, gradually forgetting how to truly enjoy life. How messed up is that?

Instead, what should really be happening – and how it used to be, before our environment became so competitive – is the following:

Our baseline should be the feeling of absolute happiness, just because we're alive. **Yes, every single person is entitled to happiness at birth.** And that's exactly why people who have had near-death experiences tend to enjoy life much more than others, because they stop taking it for granted. My point is that it's not necessary to survive a bad car accident or escape from a war, to start appreciating the fact of being alive. Because **life is the most precious gift.**

And I can teach you how to shift your baseline to the state of pure eternal happiness, with the help of neuroplasticity of your brain. It's not rocket science. It's science but it's easier than building SpaceX, I promise you. There are universal principles of how the human brain functions. There are also universal principles of what makes a human happy. Those principles have been studied and they work. And you can find them in this book in further chapters, though I wouldn't dare to consider my list of tools entirely comprehensive.

Ready to change your life?

To conclude this chapter, I would say the following.

Everything that happened to me in the last years made me realize a few things:

- Life is too short to worry about what other people think about you; what's much more important is what we think about ourselves and how we feel
- We're not as fragile as we think we are
- We can get out of any deepest shit (literally ANY) and thrive
- When we say "I can't handle this", we're lying to ourselves; we can, it's all in our heads

So if life's circumstances made you forget how to enjoy every moment of your life – read further.

What doesn't kill us – makes us stronger. Or, rather, it makes us become aware of our resilience. At the same time though, it tends to make us forget how to smile. Don't let that happen. **Get up, believe in yourself and smile. And you will get to the top of the world...** It's beautiful up here, you'll like it.

"In case of emergency"

"Pain is inevitable. Suffering is optional."
Dalai Lama

Throughout this book, we'll be talking about how to build up your "happiness baseline" that is the path to living a fulfilled joyful life, every day. Again, that doesn't mean that we are cheerful 24/7 and we don't experience negative emotions. We all do, we're humans after all and that is great, and we'll talk about that later in more detail. But when life presents us with emotional challenges and even when something significant occurs that shatters our entire universe – if our baseline is at a decent level, we will deal with it in a much healthier and stable way, without losing our identity, allowing ourselves to experience these emotions and then moving on with a smile.

I'll teach you how to build that baseline in the subsequent chapters.

But this chapter is for those who are in deep misery right now (which happens to the best of us). Before you proceed to learning the skill of eternal happiness – we need to get you out of your pain so you can actually digest the information in this book.

So those of you who are only moderately miserable – you can skip this chapter and go straight to the things that will teach you how to build your joyful "core". But keep this information handy, just in case shit hits the fan in your world. And if it does – that's okay, because you will be well equipped by then, so no big deal.

If you're one of those numerous people who recently lost something that your identity was tethered to, i.e. went through a breakup, a divorce, loss of a job, etc., and you're just in the beginning of your happiness journey and haven't yet learned to be fully sufficient and content regardless of life's circumstances (and you will, after reading this book) then here's an emergency toolkit for you to use that will help you pull yourself by you hair out of your misery (just like that fictional German character Baron Munchausen) and avoid drowning in excruciating pain.

In this chapter, we will talk about dealing with those emergency situations that throw you completely off balance, those moments when you wake up miserable and fall asleep miserable and it seems like there's no end in sight. When those things happen, it's important to avoid major mistakes that would hurt you more in the long run. So start with these tools first, and then when you're more stable – move on to the tools outlined in other chapters to get closer and closer to your goal of eternal happiness and freedom. I promise, you'll get there. But first, let's get you out of that pain.

First and foremost. Understand what caused the traumatic experience, and if there's a chance of this happening again – **get yourself out of the situation that keeps causing it.** Think about what's best for you and do it. JUST DO IT!

If the event is in the past and all you need to do now is to survive – then here's what you can do to recover.

Important. Allow yourself to immerse in your pain and truly experience it. Don't suppress. We'll talk about this in more detail in one of the chapters to come but here I'll just summarize, so you avoid hurting yourself further. Never try to pretend that nothing happened. Truly allow yourself to feel. I promise, that won't kill you. Cry when you feel like crying, scream when no one can hear you, immerse yourself for some time, allow yourself to be miserable for a few days, accept it, so then you can start letting it go.

Now, I understand (I know for a fact because I've gone through this myself) that there may be situations when you just don't seem to be able to let it go. Days go by and you feel like you're slowly fading out. You actually feel like you'd rather die because it's so painful and there's no end in sight. I have been there. Many people have been there.

It's important at this point to **not let yourself make your pain the center of your existence.** After you've allowed yourself to immerse in it for a few days – start working on letting it go, don't concentrate on it, otherwise it will start embracing you and filling up the entire space around you. Otherwise it may start to seem that it's permanent and this is how it will always be from now on and there's no escape.

If that is happening to you right now – believe me, you're not alone. Most people don't know how to deal with pain, because thanks to modern medicine, we have very limited experience with it. That's why when we face mental, or emotional, pain – we feel helpless. Many resort to taking various substances to ease it. Because we're driven by the fear of its *permanence*.

Not a surprise: alcohol helps ease the pain. The problem with it is that the effect is short-lived. The bigger problem is: when it wears off – you find yourself in a deeper black hole than you were before. So you need another dose to stop the pain, which is now greater, so you need a greater dose.

The circle continues until you become dependent on it, which happens very quickly, within a week or so. Yes, that fast. So don't do this, unless your goal is to bury yourself in a depression for life.

Here are a few ways to deal with your pain without resorting to substances and not allowing it to become a permanent part of you.

First of all, *understand that there WILL be an end.* One of the ways to do it is to imagine how you'll feel about it in 10 years. Remember: everything is temporary, though it may not seem this way now.

Second. *It's okay to ask for help.* Talk to your friends or look for a therapist.

Third. *Start writing your feelings down.* Every day. Dig it all out. Write, cry, write again, cry, feel, say what you want to say, on paper. Then burn this shit! Do this every day until you feel like there's no need to continue. You'll know when it happens.

Now, there's another powerful technique commonly used in cognitive behavior therapy called *cognitive distancing.*[14] The Distancing refers to the ability to view one's own thoughts or beliefs as "constructions of reality" rather than as reality itself.

How does cognitive distancing work? In practice, therapists ask their clients to imagine wearing colored spectacles. If you believe the world is rose-tinted or dark and gloomy because of the lenses before your eyes, that's like fusing your beliefs with reality. Realizing that the world isn't that color – just the glasses are colored – is cognitive distancing. For instance, it's like the difference between telling yourself, "Life is hard!" and "I am just assuming that life is hard." The ancient Stoics realized this fact over 2,000 years ago and it took modern therapists decades to fully understand this unique concept.

---

[14] Donald Robertson, "Cognitive Distancing in Stoicism" (2013)

Another way is to assume a *detached observer's perspective*. That's what helped me the most to deal with my pain that was following me everywhere. A variation of that can be adopting "a fly on the wall" perspective or using distant self talk: referring to yourself in a third person ("he/she", "Ira"). This actually works in situations with physical pain as well. Mentally move outside of your body, stand aside it and look at yourself from that angle (remember, it's all about perspective). You'll notice that the pain will gradually become "*foreign*", which then allows you to start seeing it as something temporary rather than overwhelmingly endless. So you start understanding that all you need to do is to observe and be patient. It's a trick you can play on your brain. Like when you're in the middle of a physical exercise and it seems like this is it, you're giving up because you have nothing left in you, but the coach yells, "Only 10 seconds left!". And as soon as you hear it, as soon as you realize that there's an end in sight – you suddenly find strength to tough it out, even though just a second ago it seemed like you were absolutely exhausted.

The same goes for pain (physical or emotional). As soon as you realize that it's not permanent – you find strength to deal with it and slowly start letting it go. And then... as you keep implementing other tools from this book, watch the pain gradually subside, day by day... until the emptiness is filled with lots of fun stuff and you find yourself an improved, better, evolved human being.

And one day the pain is completely gone, and boom – you're not an alcoholic and not mentally ill. And on top of that – you've acquired a new skill of pulling yourself out of shit by your hair, like Munhgausen. A very useful skill I have to say. After that experience, you start understanding that you *fear nothing*. You know that **whatever happens to you – you'll come out alive, reborn and of higher quality,** which ultimately allows you to live your life to the fullest, without fear, and *truly feel*. And believe me, it's much more fun that way.

For additional help dealing with non-physical pain that results from past experiences I would recommend a wonderful book by Dr. Paul Conti "Trauma: The Invisible Epidemic: How Trauma Works and How We Can Heal From It".[15] In this book Dr. Conti, a psychiatrist who completed his training at Stanford and Harvard, examines the most recent research, clinical best practices, and dozens of real-life stories to present a deeper and more urgent view of trauma. He explains how trauma affects the body and mind and proposes a set of practical tools for its treatment.

So now that we've dealt with the emergency and you're back on your feet – let's proceed to the list of tools that will allow you to build up from here, strengthen your "core" and get you on your path to becoming an eternally positive human being who **truly enjoys life, every day, regardless of the circumstances.**

---

[15] Paul Conti, "Trauma: The Invisible Epidemic: How Trauma Works and How We Can Heal From It" (2021)

Learning the skill of happiness

As mentioned earlier in this book, we tend to prioritize things in our lives that we (falsely) assume will have a positive impact on our happiness levels.

That means that you and I need to do 2 things:

1. Learn about what truly makes us happy (actions and habits that have been scientifically proven to increase life satisfaction and happiness)

2. Put them into practice

One thing you will learn from this book (as well as from Lauri Santos' Yale course "The Science of Well-Being"[16], because remember, you promised me to take it) is that just knowing about what makes you happy isn't enough to actually make you happy. As stated earlier, you actually have to put those things into practice in order to change your habits.

...And there go half of my readers who expected to receive an instant magic pill without any effort.

Now, to the other half, who are truly serious about changing their lives – let the journey begin. Remember to keep the end goal in mind. Do you want to enjoy life, every day? Do you want to wake up with a smile, knowing that the entire world's sole purpose of

---

[16] Coursera: The Science of Well-Being by Laurie Santos (offered by Yale): https://www.coursera.org/learn/the-science-of-well-being

the day is to make YOU a happy person? I'm not joking. Would you like to finally let go of your baggage, shrug off your burdens, and breathe fully and freely? Do you want to learn how to make life choices that will lead you to doing only the things that you truly enjoy, every single day?

Sounds like a decent end goal, if you ask me! Totally worth trying.

The nice thing about the concepts and tools listed in this book is that, first of all, **it's not a mysterious list. It's a very specific list that is easy to understand and implement in your life.** And second, practicing those things is actually *enjoyable*, because all of them are aimed to change your life for the better – not somebody else's life, not the lives of people around you, but YOUR life. So you will absolutely enjoy the entire process, from day one, because you will finally realize that **it's okay to treat yourself well, it's okay to love yourself and it's okay to take care of yourself before taking care of others.** Remember what flight attendants say before take off? "Put your mask on first before assisting others". Same concept.

So, for your enjoyment, and for the purpose of completely changing your life, below is the list of things, with corresponding tools and exercises, that you can start practicing today. I arranged them in the order that I find most logical, but it doesn't necessarily mean that the later ones are any less important. Personally, I still practice all of them. You can start with the ones that seem most natural to you and, once they turn into effortless habits, pick up another one, then another one, until you learn them all and they all become part of your existence. I guarantee that you will feel the difference within a month.

Happy reading. And happy life to you.

1. Self-acceptance and self-esteem

"We don't have to wait until we are on our deathbed
to realize what a waste of our precious lives it is
to carry the belief that something is wrong with us."

Tara Brach

There's a reason why this item is occupying the honorable first place on this list.

I've recently discovered that many psychological problems stem from low self-esteem that, in turn, stem from problems with self-acceptance. Should've learned this earlier in life, but better late than never... The feeling of self-worth comes from true unconditional love for yourself (self-acceptance), which is dependent on being able to be true to yourself, regardless of how other people perceive you.

Being true to yourself means not doing things that others expect you to do if that hurts you or contradicts your beliefs. It means to never lie to yourself.

Being true to yourself means accepting who you really are and not what others think you should be. It means to not pretend to be someone else in order to gain acceptance from others. Instead, you need to **accept yourself**, everything in yourself: perceived good and perceived bad.

That's why **what you think about yourself is way more critical than what others think about you.** And more importantly: how you feel about yourself shouldn't be *dependent* on what other people think about you.

Look at it this way: the size of your butt doesn't fluctuate with other people's opinion. It is what it is, regardless of the assessment from the outside. The fact that somebody thinks it's too big, or you think they think it's too big, which is even worse – is just a subjective opinion that has nothing to do with real facts and this should have nothing to do with how you should feel about yourself.

When I was growing up, I was very insecure about the fact that my legs were short. Then I realized that my (subjectively) short legs didn't prevent me from doing awesome things, reaching my goals, being liked and, moreover, being loved. In fact, one of my favorite psychologists Michail Labkovskiy said in his book "I want and I will" (which is unfortunately only published in Russian[17]) that the following 3 things don't really matter when it comes to falling in love: age, appearance and weight. So I stopped worrying about my legs, and only later discovered that they're actually standard.

So, the moral of the story: it's really all about the reference point ("my butt is bigger than the girl's who's advertising Victoria's Secret underwear"), which is really *entirely* in our heads.

Accept yourself. Together with your butt, your legs, your thoughts, your previous actions, your traumas, and every other piece of you, inside and out. Self-acceptance is **unconditional**. To be self-accepting is to feel satisfied with who you are, despite perceived flaws and regardless of past choices. According to Russell Grieger, a clinical psychologist and professor at the University of Virginia, unconditional self-acceptance is understanding that you are separate from your actions and your qualities.[18]

---

[17] Mihail Labkovskij, "Hochu i budu. Prinjat' sebja, poljubit' zhizn' i stat' schastlivym" (2017)

[18] Russell Grieger, "Be Perfectly Imperfect" (2013)

1. Self-acceptance and self-esteem

As it turns out, self-acceptance is not an automatic or default state. Many of us have trouble accepting ourselves exactly as we are. When you practice unconditional self-acceptance, you can begin to love yourself, embrace your authentic self, and work on continuously improving, to be a better version of yourself, every day.

And get this. If you **love YOU, you will be capable of truly loving others** – not being addicted, not being dependent or possessive, but truly loving, in a healthy way. Also, if you accept yourself and stop pretending to be someone else – you will attract people who admire you for who you are. And those who don't accept you this way – are not required to stick around.

Self-acceptance absolutely **affects the quality of your relationships with other people** and whether those relationships are defined by drama (if your reactions are driven by childhood trauma and insecurities) or by healthy common sense (if you embrace yourself fully and react to other people and their actions in an adequate manner without "reading between the lines").

Let me explain.

You may have noticed that different people may react differently to the same situation. One person may completely disregard a comment made by a friend, while another, triggered by a past trauma or insecurity, will view it as a threat to their personal qualities or even as an insult, cease speaking to the friend who made the comment, and possibly even end the friendship.

To paint a clearer picture, here are a few real-life examples of such situations with different reactions to the same comment.

Situation #1

– Friend: "Are you taking this vacation alone? Where are your kids?"

– Me being insecure about how much time I dedicate to my children: "Are you saying I'm a bad mother?? Look who's talking!!"

– Friend: "Jeez, relax. I didn't mean that at all."

End of the friendship.

..•..

– Friend: "Are you taking this vacation alone? Where are your kids?"

– Me after working on my self-acceptance: "Yeah I've been working my ass off and really need some time alone, I totally deserve it."

– Friend: "Damn, girl, I absolutely agree with you. You're my hero! I should do the same."

Friendship continues, the friend does the same, is grateful to you for being her role model, her life improves, everyone is happy.

Situation #2

– Friend: "Your shirt seems a bit too tight."

– A person who is insecure about his body: "Are you saying I'm fat?? Have you seen yourself in the mirror lately??"

Continues watching Netflix and getting fatter and grumpier, while losing friends one by one.

..•..

– Friend: "Your shirt seems a bit too tight."

– A person with good self-esteem and self-acceptance: "Oh thanks, I appreciate it. Sounds like I need to hit the gym again."

Goes to the gym and works on his body or buys a bigger shirt and feels great about himself (both are equally adequate, as long as he's happy at the end of the day).

You get the point. It's all in our heads. **It's the reactions to circumstances that shape our lives, it's not the circumstances themselves.**

1. Self-acceptance and self-esteem

I can't overstate the importance of this: self-acceptance is essential for your happiness but what's equally important is that it also allows your friends and significant others to be open and honest with you instead of constantly walking on eggshells or even hiding things from you in fear of causing drama. **That allows you to have deeper, more meaningful connections with others.** And, as a result, will make you, and them, happier.

Keep in mind that it doesn't mean that people who are "not easily offended" take crap from others and can't defend themselves. It's actually just the opposite. We take things for what they are, we are objective in our assessment of the situation and, if the situation is not favorable for us, we walk away, without drama and attacks.

So, if you want to live a high-quality, happy life – be who you are. And accept it. It doesn't mean you shouldn't have personal goals. You should absolutely strive to become a better version of yourself, every day (because it's just much more fun that way). What it means is that instead of waiting to start loving yourself only when you become perfect (and sorry to break it to you, that'll never happen) you admit that you're a work-in-progress and that you love yourself the way you are.

Now, self-acceptance is not identical to self-esteem, though they're very closely related. According to Positive Psychology, "self-esteem refers to how you feel about yourself – whether you feel you are generally good, worthwhile, and valuable – while self-acceptance is simply acknowledging and accepting that you are who you are."[19] In other words, in addition to loving yourself, you also *know* that today, as a work-in-progress masterpiece, you're already quite awesome, and tomorrow you'll be even better.

---

[19] Positive Psychology: Self-Acceptance (March 2022): https://positivepsychology.com/self-acceptance/

Full self-acceptance can lay the foundation for positive self-esteem, and the two frequently go hand-in-hand. Self-esteem stems from self-acceptance, which ultimately results in you being a much healthier (mentally healthier) human being.

Now that we've gone through the background concepts of self-acceptance that have hopefully helped you *understand* the importance of self-acceptance and self-love, here are the things you can *practice* on a daily basis to improve your feeling of self-worth.

● EXERCISES

DO THIS TODAY:

Self-acceptance worksheet

Fill out the self-acceptance worksheet[20] below.

The point of the worksheet is to focus on the "good" things about yourself. I'm using the word "good" in quotes for a reason. Because again, the notion of "goodness" is subjective: what's good for you may not necessarily be good for another person. So here we're talking about the things that you subjectively consider good: the things you like about yourself, things you implement in your life that you appreciate and honor about yourself.

---

[20] Susyn Reeve, Joan Breiner, "How to Love Yourself Worksheet" (2009): http://www.self-esteem-experts.com/support-files/ howtoloveyourselfworksheet.pdf

1. Self-acceptance and self-esteem

Here is the list of questions you need to answer:

1. What do I appreciate about who I am?
2. What are my strengths?
3. What do my friends appreciate about me?
4. What do I like about others? Which of these attributes do I possess?
5. How would people who love me describe me?

When you have completed your list, read it aloud while looking in a mirror.

1. Begin each statement with the words, "[Your name], I love your..." (e.g., "Ira, I love your sense of humor! Ira, I love your willingness to help others!").
2. Begin each statement with the words, "I love my..." (e.g., "I love my commitment to feeling good about myself! I love my openness to learn new things!").

The goal of this worksheet is to help you start to open yourself up to the "good" aspects of yourself rather than the "bad" (or, rather, the ones you perceive as bad, or the ones you think society perceives as bad). Self-acceptance implies acknowledging and accepting both the positive and negative aspects of yourself, and maintaining a healthy balance in your attention to them.

DO THIS EVERY DAY FOR AT LEAST A WEEK:

1. In the morning when you wake up, look in the mirror, hug yourself and truly accept the unique, wonderful work-in-progress person staring back at you. Nobody is perfect... though, perfection is a very relative and subjective concept, as well as the entire concept of "good and bad" and morality in general, we'll talk about it later in the book. What matters is that you know deep in your heart that you want to do good

things for others. And if you haven't yet realized it yourself, I'll explain to you why, in one of the following chapters. In any case, you're just an awesome human being, I know that for a fact and you should know that, too.

2. Keep reminding yourself that your actions don't define you as a person (a good one or a bad one).

OTHER HELPFUL TOOLS:

1. Maintaining self-esteem

Even if our self-esteem levels are generally high, sometimes we find ourselves in situations when we start questioning our own integrity. Some experience this more often than others. One of the tools that I found useful when experiencing moments of weakness with low self-esteem is the following.

Whenever you do something you're proud of, or hear/read something about yourself where someone else (your friends, your parents, your employer, whoever is important in your life) thinks and talks highly of you – make a record of it. Take a screenshot, write it down, save it in a folder. I keep mine on my phone for easy access, I called it "affirmations". So when something happens in my life that shatters my self-esteem and I feel like a total loser, I swipe through the screenshots in that folder that contain actual facts about me being totally awesome, successful, talented and worthy of being a role-model for many. How it works is: because you can't argue with the facts that stare at you from the screen, you quickly realize that this moment of weakness was just a temporary glitch in your system of self-worth and is not something that defines you. This exercise absolutely helps you go back to a healthy self-esteem level and move on with your happy life.

1. Self-acceptance and self-esteem

...And yes, after all my achievements I still feel insecure at times, though not nearly as often as before. I'm still human after all, and I accept it... Thankfully, I know how to deal with that and I hope these tools will help you do the same.

2. Minimizing social media influence

Spend less time following other people's lives on social media. I'm serious. There have been studies[21] that discovered a negative correlation between levels of self-esteem and Facebook use, through the mechanism of social comparison that we spoke about earlier. The less you care about other people's achievements, the happier you will be. Remember, they only post great things that happen to them (I do, too), and you don't know what's really going on in their lives.

To reiterate: **if you truly embrace and love yourself, then your happiness and your self-sufficiency won't rely on anyone or anything outside of your own head.** You'll just be a much healthier and happier individual because that's what everything stems from. I know it's easier said than done. That's why what you need to do is start practicing these tools today to see the results. You will see them, I promise, in as little as just a few weeks.

And it's never too late to start truly loving yourself. Self-love is an essential element of happiness. Forget the brainwashing about self-sacrifice for the sake of the greater good. You are the most important thing in your life and you need to take care of YOU. This is not selfishness. This is self-awareness. Which, in turn, benefits other people around you.

---

[21] E. A. Vogel et al, "Social comparison, social media, and self-esteem. Psychology of Popular Media Culture" (2014)

If you have someone else you need to take care of – it's even more important to start with yourself. Nobody will benefit from an exhausted, helpless person who has nothing to give: your children, significant others, relatives, friends, your employer and the society in general.

Take good care of yourself, love yourself, embrace yourself.

You're not defined by your past actions and YOU are the best thing that ever happened in your life.

2. Lack of judgment

> "The self-righteous scream judgments against others
> to hide the noise of skeletons dancing in their own closets."
> *John Mark Green*

The concept of judgment (or lack thereof) is closely related to self-acceptance and the "reference point" that I mentioned earlier in the introduction chapter. Just like you shouldn't judge yourself, you also should refrain from judging others.

Let me start by saying this, which may sound like common sense: everyone is different and everyone is awesome in their own way.

What logically follows is that there are no "good" or "bad" people. Each of us has both attractive traits and also those that are perceived as unattractive, which does not mean they are bad. They may just be inconvenient for others, and mainly – because those other people have their own triggers and insecurities.

For example, a teenager who just can't seem to learn how to clean his room without constant reminders (or even threats) from his parents, who picked up smoking from his peers and brings home low grades from school. Is he a bad person? I bet you can find people in his circle who think the world of him. He's just unorganized and doesn't fit the "ideal" image of a child that his parents had in mind – a nerd who has the potential to become a lawyer or a doctor. It's inconvenient for his parents, but guess what, he might become a businessman making 10x what lawyers make and he'll be a happier person, if his parents stop judging him. On another note, happiness is not correlated to income, we'll talk about it in one of the future chapters.

Another example: a husband who has an alcohol addiction. Is he a bad person? His addiction doesn't bother him or his friends who keep him company. It bothers his wife who has an option of either sticking around and being unhappy, or leaving him. However, the act of drinking doesn't define the husband as a bad person. He could be an angel for all I know, ready to give his last dollar to a homeless person.

In any case, what I'm trying to say is that "positive and negative" are subjective and relative concepts. So instead of labeling people as "good" or "bad" – how about letting them live their own lives without judging them? You'd want others to do the same for you, right?

If a particular habit or an action by another person is inconvenient to you – feel free to express it (in a respectful way, with no drama or attacks, which you will be able to do if you have reached a decent level of self-acceptance after practicing the tools in the previous chapter) and if it doesn't lead to any changes of that person's behavior – walk away and don't interact with them if you absolutely can't tolerate that habit. Don't judge and don't try to change him/her. They might be absolutely happy with who they are, as they should be.

Long story short: there's no universal criteria for a "norm" that would help define deviations as "bad". Everyone has their opinion and their view on things. That opinion is a derivative of many factors: cultural (what seems appropriate in some cultures may be frowned upon in others, like in Singapore you can go to jail for chewing gum), generational (things change a lot overtime and with that, our values and principles change, take gay marriages for example) and personal (the way a person was raised, the environment he/she was exposed to, their personal life story), etc.

What I'm trying to say is that it means that "norms" and "adequateness" are artificial and relative, and there's no universal rule of what's normal and what's not, what's good and what's bad.

That's exactly why people who travel a lot tend to be much more flexible and less judgmental. One of the reasons why I love traveling is that it shows you, again and again, that things that are considered weird where you live may be absolutely normal somewhere else. And that opens up your horizons and stretches your mind. That's how you learn to never judge. Because, again, normality is very subjective.

Why am I telling you all this? Because **learning to accept people for who they are (lack of judgment) provides an incredible feeling of liberation that is almost as strong as after you learn to accept yourself, which ultimately increases your happiness levels.** Remember, you're doing it for yourself still, not for others. Others will absolutely benefit if you stop trying to change them, but first of all, it will make YOU a happier person.

Don't judge. You never know the true reason of any person's behavior. You never know what's truly in their heads.

● EXERCISES

DO THIS EVERY DAY FOR AT LEAST A WEEK:

Observing your thoughts and developing self-awareness

The very first step to stop being judgmental is to catch yourself in the act. This cannot be achieved at one go and requires practice and some self-awareness. Try to observe your thoughts and when you catch yourself being critical about others, start questioning yourself. Ask yourself, first of all, why are you triggered by this specific behavior/action of the other person? Is there a problem in your own head that causes this negative reaction? Consider if you or the other person will benefit from your judgment.

OTHER HELPFUL TOOLS:

1. Practice empathy

You can never know why some people behave a certain way. They might be dealing with something, consciously or unconsciously. A bad day? A bad life?

Show some empathy, even if you are not aware of the other person's situation. Try to understand the other person's behavior.

2. Be curious rather than critical

Curiosity can be a great tool to overcome a judgmental attitude. Try to be more curious about something you don't understand instead of being too critical. Explore the reasons behind a certain behavior instead of dwelling on the negative points.

3. Travel more

Make an effort to notice things in other cultures that are different from what you're accustomed to.

If you can't travel for any reason – expand your social circle. Hanging out with diverse groups of people and expanding your social circle can help you stay open-minded. Try to interact with people who are different from you, be it in race, culture, interest, careers, or ideas. Being around people with different beliefs, perspectives and backgrounds will help you become more understanding and open-minded as you will learn about the challenges that others face.

3. Sorting your life

There's a technique in agile software development called "Start, Stop, Continue". It's used in retrospective meetings that are held after a development iteration, called "sprint". There's a lot to learn from it, for our daily life. Every human needs a "retrospective" on a regular basis.

During the retrospective, one reflects on what happened in the last "iteration" and identifies actions for improvement going forward.

Start, Stop, Continue is an action-oriented technique. It makes you focus on creating a list of concrete actions by looking back at the last sprint while also looking forward to the next.

Using the same analogy, we need to run periodic retrospectives of ourselves and our lives, do a cleanup, reorganize and optimize. We need to look back, reassess our life and make decisions to:

- *Stop* – what makes us unhappy and adds stress (commitments, routines, jobs, relationships);

- *Continue* – what is truly important, what strengthens our integrity, what makes us better humans in our own perception;

- *Start* – new things that make us happier, more complete, that give us energy to evolve and become better versions of ourselves, every day.

Some people implement this with the help of New Year's resolutions. My sprints, however, always tend to start and end in summer, which probably takes its roots from the school year pattern, which dictated the date my new life started (May 28, 2004 at LAX Tom Bradley International Terminal where I arrived from Belarus with a suitcase and a backpack) and set the tone for all future "sprints".

People who travel a lot have an advantage of more frequent "retrospectives" (I revise my life every time I come back from an international trip). But most get buried in their daily routines, get stuck in commitments and responsibilities that are no longer enjoyable, adapting themselves to their lifestyle instead of trying to adapt and reorganize their lives. Reason being: as humans, we're afraid of change, of the unknown. We're also afraid of being judged.

If you just recognized yourself in that last paragraph – read further, you're in for a treat.

In reality, **most changes happen for the best and make us better, stronger and happier.**

Don't be afraid of changes or being judged by others. Because judgment is bullshit, as we recently learned, and progress is life.

And here are the best ways to change your life for the better. Have fun.

● EXERCISES

DO THIS TODAY:

"Sorting your life"

This is one of the most life-changing exercises you'll ever go through.

Step 1: take a large piece of paper, divide it into two parts

Step 2: on the left side – write down things (actions, people) that give you energy, that make you feel better and more complete, even for a short period of time; on the right side – write down everything that takes your energy away from you, what makes you feel down and adds stress.

It's important to be honest with yourself about what you TRULY enjoy and what you TRULY find draining. Nobody will see the list except for you. You can burn it later if you'd like. It might take a bit of time to dig things out of the deeper levels of your psyche. Normally, the things that come out last are the ones that are really true and really deep. So make it a point to have a list of at least 20 items in each category.

Step 3: In your daily life, start concentrating on doing things from the left side that give you energy and avoid doing things that make you suffer. Done. Simple as that.

For example, when going through this exercise, I discovered that things that make me very happy are: exercising, driving when listening to loud music, and sitting on a beach staring at the ocean with a cup of coffee in my hand (as seen on the cover of this book).Yes, it can be those little things!!! It doesn't have to be "buying a house", "buying new boobs" or "getting married". So I made sure to allocate time every week to do those little things. Boy, did it change my life!

This is an incredible exercise that, alone, can make a huge difference in your energy levels and your life satisfaction. And no, it's not enough to formulate these things in your head. I can hear that little voice saying: "Yeah, I already know what those things are, there's no need for me to spend time on writing them down". Believe me, you'll be surprised to see what you dig out after spending at least 30 minutes on the list and being 100 percent honest with yourself. There will be things on that page that you had no idea about or were never brave enough to admit. Writing it down is a gazillion percent more effective than just thinking about it.

Beware: this exercise may make you reconsider your friendships. You may have heard the phrase "you're an average of your 5 friends". Indeed you are. Ask yourself: "Who are my 5 closest friends that I spend the most time with?", "Do they make me feel good about myself?", "Do I want to be like them?". And then act accordingly.

Clearly understanding what parts of your life make you happy and unhappy is half of your success and is a big step towards the new YOU. And don't be surprised if you find your spouse in the "energy sucking" list...

¯_(ツ)_/¯

The second half of the success – is actually implementing it in your daily life. And that may mean breaking relationships or quitting a job. I'm not suggesting anything specific... Actually, yes I am. If your therapist can't take the responsibility for suggesting this – I will. If you are in a relationship (personal or professional) that makes you miserable – get out of it. Stop torturing yourself
54

and your partner, or your employer. Is this really how you want to spend the rest of your life? Several years ago, I quit my job after realizing I was in the wrong place. I found another one within a month and it paid double my previous salary and was a much better fit for me as a person and as a professional.

Give yourself a chance to feel alive again. Alive, respected and loved. You deserve it.

DO THIS EVERY DAY FOR AT LEAST A MONTH:

"Finding time affluence"

Another very important tool. Allocate time for yourself! And, what's more important: when you do – stop feeling guilty about it. Self-care is not selfish! No more "why am I sitting on my ass while laundry is still sitting in a pile next to the washing machine?" #beentheredonethat

Step 1: When planning your week, first add events that will allow you to take care of *yourself* (a manicure, gym, a quiet walk in the park, a nap, meditation, a cup of coffee with a friend – whatever floats your boat) and only then add other tasks and responsibilities to your calendar. If you do it in a reverse order – chances are, you'll never be able to squeeze any "me time" into your busy schedule. I'm sure you've seen this happen over and over again, week after week.

Clue: things to add in the "me time" are the ones you discover in the left column of the page from the previous exercise!

Step 2: Actually stick to that schedule. Don't find excuses why you can't do it. *Learn* to allocate time for yourself, even if it may seem like you don't have any free time. I don't believe you! It's really just a matter of priorities.

And if you're not yet convinced that free time is important – here's what smart people say about it. A study[22] was conducted in 2016 that discovered that people who value time are happier than those who value money. So there you go. A no-brainer.

Invest in time affluence! It might not seem natural in the beginning (especially if you're a parent) but, believe me, you'll quickly find it very rewarding. If you devote some time to yourself, you'll have more energy for others. You'll have much more to give. I promise you. You'll notice how stress goes away, how kids suddenly start behaving, how your spouse becomes less grumpy. It's because YOU become calmer, more peaceful and satisfied. Your loved ones will immediately feel it, most likely without even realizing it (so you don't even have to tell them that you take yoga classes every Sunday – it will be our little secret).

Reorganize your routine in a way that puts you at the top of your list of "important things in life".

---

[22] Hal E. Hershfield et al, "People Who Choose Time Over Money Are Happier" (2016)

4. Recognizing your emotions

"Instead of resisting any emotion, the best way to dispel it is to enter it fully, embrace it and see through your resistance."

Deepak Chopra

"You're so strong," – I've heard many times in the last few years. I would agree. But it hasn't always been this way. It took me a while to get there.

So what makes me strong and resilient? What makes me realize that I can get out of any deepest shit, which ultimately allows me to live my life to the fullest, without any fear?

I'm strong because I'm not afraid of my emotions. It doesn't mean I don't feel them. I just accept them, whatever they are. I can't say I'm not afraid of anything. What I can say is that I'm not afraid of being afraid, or hurt, or sad, or loved, or being in love.

I embrace *positive* emotions or, rather, what we humans label as "positive". But I'm also aware of their temporary nature. So I embrace experiences that make me happy and evoke positive emotions because I'm not afraid of being sad when they're gone.

I also equally embrace *negative* emotions because they can, and should, be used as a chance to evolve. When you experience them, you can use that to learn more about yourself, if you treat it as a lesson.

I have learned to recognize my emotions and not be afraid of them because they always pass. It's all about perspective. And this chapter, including the tools in it, will help you find that perspective.

You will learn to recognize your emotions and not be afraid of them because (please pay attention here):

– There are no "bad" or "wrong" emotions or feelings

– Everything is temporary

Again, it's all entirely in our own heads. The tools from this chapter will help you put things in perspective, which will allow you to embrace your emotions, whatever they may be and, as a result, live a much happier and fulfilled life.

Let me give you more context, for better understanding.

We go through a lot in our lives. We have different experiences. Good and bad. Wonderful, exciting, amazing, challenging, sad, frightening, breaking, healing, boring, depressing, surprising. Different experiences evoke different emotions. **They are part of us and it's okay.**

Different people have different triggers and different sensitivity levels. For example, for some, a break up may be the end of the world, especially if their entire identity was tethered to their partner. Others may tolerate it easily. So when you see a person having a hard time dealing with something – please refrain from judging and telling them to toughen up ("Wipe your tears, be a man!"). First of all, you don't know what they're really going through. And second, that's not what they need to hear. Even if it temporarily helps them calm down – that's because they just suppressed what they were feeling, shoved it deeper into their subconsciousness, only for that dark shadow to slowly keep growing in the back of their minds and one day blow up in their face when they least expect it. And they'll be wondering "what did just happen?" and "where did that come from?". Well, it's because some time ago, they were told that what they were feeling was "not good" and "not worthy" so they didn't have a chance to process it in a healthy way.

I beg you: Don't do it to your friends. Don't do it to your children. Don't do it to yourself!

First of all. Again, there are no "bad" or "wrong" emotions. We have the right and the reason to feel what we feel at any point in time. The worst thing you can do is to suppress your emotions. The worst thing you can do to others (especially your kids, if you have them) is to make them feel bad about feeling.

Second, everything is temporary. EVERYTHING. Events, emotions, life itself.

We all know this. It's a simple fact. But for some reason, we treat those things above as if we weren't aware of their temporary nature.

When we encounter negative feelings or emotions – we tend to do 2 things:

- Suppress (as described above), because they scare us, we're afraid that this pain will stay with us forever. We think these feelings are wrong and we don't want to have anything to do with them. So we choose to pretend we never felt them and hide them deeeeep inside.

- Or, another extreme: we get stuck and concentrate on them. By doing this, we push ourselves deeper and deeper into the black hole. Some start doing drugs or drinking. And the black hole expands. The pain gets worse because we make it worse.

Instead, the healthy approach would be to: **recognize what you're feeling, label it, realize that there *will* be an end** (this will help eliminate the fear factor), **face it, accept it, allow yourself to truly *feel*** (I promise, you won't die!), **and then see it leave your mind and body.** You may need to do this a few times, depending on the strength of the emotion and how deep the trigger is. You may need to scream when you're alone in your car, you may need to cry your eyes out when taking a shower and nobody's watching. You may need to punch a wall. It's okay. It's absolutely okay. Allow yourself to feel.

If you had a life-shattering event and your pain is strong, just remember: tomorrow will be another day. And then there will be another one and another one. Keep breathing, keep reading this book (you can also reread the chapter "In case of emergency"), keep practicing these tools, and the pain will eventually subside. If it surfaces again – don't push it away, immerse in it, again, allow yourself to feel, then slowly let it go, don't concentrate on it, live your life. And one day the pain will go away completely. It always does, if you do things right, if you process it in a healthy way. And the sooner you realize this and start working towards a healthier YOU, the quicker you recover.

A good friend once told me when I was going through tough times: "A year from now you won't even remember what you're worried about right now". At that time, the problem I was dealing with seemed like the end of the world to me, so I didn't believe him. But he was right.

If you look back at your life a year ago, a few years ago, you will remember those moments that caused pain or anxiety. What you will also notice is that the pain, the worries, the sadness did go away. If not yet – they will soon. Practice tools from this book. You'll be a new person in less than a month.

4. Recognizing your emotions

Instead of suppressing, or getting stuck in negativism, or becoming a shadow and watching days go by, we should learn how to truly feel and live our life to the fullest.

Because life is also temporary.

● EXERCISES

DO THIS TODAY:

Emotions journal

This is one of those must-have, life-changing tools that are ridiculously simple yet insanely effective.

Every night, before you go to bed, make a note of how you're feeling. There's an app for that (probably multiple apps, but I just use "Calm"). Install it *right now* and set the emotions journal reminder for, let's say, 9pm – that's it. Now you don't have to remember, your phone will do it all for you. And when it asks you "How are you feeling?" – just make sure to be honest with yourself. Remember it's OKAY to be sad, or angry, or scared, or tired or anything else that you may feel. Record it. Do it every day. I've been doing it for almost a year and I can say this is one of the most effective daily tools in my arsenal.

What does it do and why is it so powerful? The information it imparts to you is multi-faceted. First of all, it teaches you to *recognize your emotions and be honest about it.* It teaches you to *be okay with any of the emotions on the list.* There's a choice of at least 10, "positive" and "negative" ones. Because it's impossible to be happy 365 days of the year and it's okay to feel sad or stressed or tired! It's totally normal! It also teaches you to give them a name. And last but not least... drum rolls: it gives you PERSPECTIVE.

Here's the magic. Once you've recorded your emotional state for some period of time, let's say a month, you can go back and review the history. First of all, you will see how your mental state improves over time (there's no way it won't, after you've read this book), which on its own makes you feel great about yourself. Second, what's more important, it shows you that negative emotions don't last forever. *They're temporary.* You may be sad for a few days but then it's replaced by a feeling of joy or excitement, or happiness, and you have a row of smiley faces in your "emotions calendar".

Why is it so life-changing? When you truly realize that all emotions are okay and all of them are temporary (you'll see it with your own eyes), next time you feel sad, you'll know that tomorrow will be another day and you'll smile again. So you'll embrace your sadness and won't run away from it, allowing yourself to face it, feel it and then truly let it go, thus becoming a much healthier (mentally healthier) individual.

DO THIS EVERY DAY FOR AT LEAST A WEEK:

Labeling feelings, allowing yourself to feel, recognizing your emotions

A quick and simple exercise that can help you be more aware of what is really happening inside of you and learning to let go without getting stuck or suppressing.

When you feel a strong emotion (normally we want to work on the ones we label as "negative"), stop whatever you're doing (unless you're on the freeway) because you don't want to lose it, you want to catch it by its tail before it escapes. And I know you've already mastered the skill of suppressing so it might escape very quickly – so catch it quick! At that moment, you may not even have an understanding of what it is exactly, you just feel it somewhere in your body (mine normally concentrates in the chest). FYI, based on what we know from modern science, we cannot say that emotions arise and sit just in our heads. They involve a host of biological events in your entire ecosystem, that's why you can feel them (if you pay attention) in different parts of your body: stomach, chest, throat, etc. If you learn to recognize that feeling, it will be easier to recognize your emotions.

Try to pull the "tail" of that feeling and that emotion and intensify it, so you can label it: sadness, jealousy, fear, anger... It's important to give it a name, to identify it, because that makes it more "material" and allows you to "work" with it.

Try to understand what caused it. An event, somebody's comment, somebody's actions, or lack thereof. It's important to get as close to the root as possible.

Allow yourself to *immerse* in it. Feel it. Feel it with your entire heart, your entire body. It's important to not resist, not build barriers to protect yourself from it. Just know that truly feeling it won't kill you, it will liberate you. Intensify it, really *allow* yourself to feel. Scream if you need to (preferably when nobody can hear you), punch a wall, cry, cringe, run, whatever your body wants to do to let it out. If you're not alone – you may flex your muscles for example, or do something else that is subtle and unnoticable.

Let it go and feel liberated. That's it. If it comes back – do it again. Practice it regularly and you'll be much more in tune with and in control of your inner world without gathering piles of growing dark energy balls in the back of your mind. #beentheredonethat

OTHER HELPFUL TOOLS:

"Head, Heart, Instincts" technique

I would also like to introduce you to a technique that I found extremely helpful for dealing with my emotions "in the moment" and that I personally use quite often. Its author is an amazing practicing psychologist, Irina Maslova-Semenova who invented her own method for the study of psychosomatics and childhood traumas in adults and recently published a book "The Genesis Method: love yourself more than you love your family and your job"[23], which is unfortunately, only available in Russian, so far.

The name of the technique is "Head. Heart. Instincts.". If you speak Russian – you can watch this public video[24] (see the reference in the footnote) where it is explained in detail.

I'm taking the liberty of translating the mechanism of this technique into English from the original language, for my readers.

The goal of this tool is to help "work" on your emotions and reactions that arise in stressful situations. The underlying concept is that our reactions to certain events in our adult life stem from our childhood, so the technique allows you to remove that connection between the negative self-definition and your reactions/emotions as an adult. It teaches you to choose a healthier strategy of dealing

---

[23] Irina Maslova, "Metod 'Genezis" (2021)

[24] Irina Maslova-Semenova: Stressful Situations. How to work on your emotions (2019): https://www.youtube.com/watch?v=DFD__tudRqg

with the situation in the moment as well as afterwards, thus allowing you to, first of all, recognize emotions, face them, and let them go without getting stuck or suppressing.

Step 1: Remember a situation that caused the emotion you'd like to "deal with". Pick something recent.

Step 2: Close your eyes. Put your hand on your head and say to yourself: "I accept my thoughts". With that, restore the situation in your memory: what you were thinking then and there, remember and imagine again what was happening.

Step 3: Inhale deeply. On the exhale, move your attention to your heart, put your hand on your chest and say to yourself: "I accept my feelings". With that, restore in your memory those emotions that were caused by the situation. Allow them to intensify. "I'm allowing myself to feel, it is safe for me". Keep intensifying the emotion/feeling. Identify it, label it. What is it? Sadness, anger, fear? Give it a name.

Step 4: Move your hand to your stomach. Say to yourself: "I accept my instincts". Find the stress at the bottom of your abdomen – the particular instinct that feeds that specific emotion and doesn't allow you to fully free yourself from it. What is it? Identify the instinct. Is it a desire to run away, or attack, or hide, or cringe into a tiny ball and freeze? What does your body want to do in this moment? Imagine you're there, in the situation and this is happening to you right now.

Step 5: Keep your hand on your stomach and say:

(using the example of instinct to attack)

"I recognize my instinct to attack

I recognize that my instinct to attack ensures my survival

I recognize that my instinct to attack ensures my safety

I recognize the difference between attacking and surviving

I recognize the difference between attacking and safety

I recognize all my traumas, starting with the first one related to the instinct to attack

I am not defined by the instinct to attack

My identity is not defined by the instinct to attack

I'm allowing changes to happen right now. I feel the changes inside me."

I recommend going through this technique at least 5 times (using different situations from the recent past), so that you can memorize the steps and go through it quickly and easily when needed. The whole thing takes maybe 30 seconds once you master it and may be very useful "in the moment" when you need help dealing with your reactions to a certain situation, like screaming at your kids when they misbehave and causing more psychological traumas for the younger generation.

5. Gratitude

*"It's not joy that makes us grateful,
it's gratitude that makes us joyful."*
David Steindl-Rast

One of the first epiphanies I had when learning about the mechanism of happiness is that being grateful for little things, and people, in your life and actually training your brain to register those things is one of the most crucial elements of developing your new "happy" baseline.

It's a pretty simple concept, and so are the supplied exercises, but it's very powerful.

Gratitude is a positive emotional state in which one recognizes and appreciates what one has received in life. Research shows that taking time to experience, as well as express gratitude makes you happier and even healthier.

The simple act of registering and experiencing gratitude has a host of positive benefits: it can increase your mood and lower your stress levels, it can even strengthen your immune system and lower your blood pressure. Experiencing gratitude also can make you feel a stronger social connection, which makes you, and others, happier.

Dr. Brené Brown, Research Professor at the University of Houston, once shared: "The relationship between joy and gratitude was one of the important things I found in my research. I wasn't expecting it. In my 12 years of research on 11,000 pieces of data,

I did not interview one person who had described themselves as joyful, who also did not actively practice gratitude."[25]

By the way, Dr. Brené Brown is also the author of one of the best books I've recently read – "Daring Greatly"[26]. Highly recommend.

Long story short: practicing gratitude invites joy into our lives. And who doesn't want to be joyful? #no-brainer

● EXERCISES

DO THIS TODAY:

Gratitude letter/visit

This tool is taken from Lauri Santos' Yale course "The Science of Well-Being".[27] Beware: research suggests that this exercise will have a big impact on your happiness and that of another person.

Write a letter of gratitude to someone you care about. For this assignment, think of one living person who has made a big difference in your life, but whom you never properly thanked. Then find a quiet spot when you have a half-hour free and write a heartfelt letter to that person explaining how he or she has touched your life and why he or she is meaningful to you. Your letter can be as long as you want, but try to make it at least 300 words or so.

---

[25] Brené Brown, "Joy and Gratitude" (2018): https://globalleadership.org/articles/leading-yourself/brene-brown-on-joy-and-gratitude/

[26] Brené Brown, "Daring Greatly: How the Courage to Be Vulnerable Transforms the Way We Live, Love, Parent, and Lead" (2015)

[27] Coursera: The Science of Well-Being by Laurie Santos (offered by Yale): https://www.coursera.org/learn/the-science-of-well-being

Then you must deliver that letter to the person in question. Just say you want to talk without explaining why. You could read the letter to them over the phone or Skype, but for an extra huge happiness boost, it's definitely recommended scheduling a time to visit them in person to share your letter. However you meet up, you should read it aloud. Make sure to have some tissues handy for this one. A gratitude letter is one of the most powerful tools for increasing happiness because it can forge social bonds and really change someone's life.

Indeed it does. When I went through this exercise, I cried my eyes out, twice. First time – when writing the letter, the second time – when giving it to the recipient. I had a great deal of gratitude towards that person for many years before I did this. But because I was born in the Soviet Union and we, Soviet people, are not taught to express emotions, I never told him how I felt. I mean, he probably knew, it was visible on the surface and through my actions, but I never really told him. And I was tortured by this feeling of something unaccomplished, undone...This exercise made me gather my guts, write it all down (I had a total of 6 pages... because you know, I have this thing for writing...) and hand it to him (the Soviet in me unfortunately prevented me from reading it to him outloud). Boy, was it transformational... It changed me and I'm sure it changed him. It made our bond even stronger. And even though we never talked about it again, I know that he knows, and that makes me feel absolutely happy.

DO THIS EVERY DAY FOR AT LEAST A MONTH:

Daily gratitude journal

Another one that is ridiculously simple yet outrageously effective. PROMISE ME YOU'LL DO IT!!! On a daily basis, record three things that you're grateful for today. There is an app for that. Again, I use "Calm" but you can pick the one you like.

Install it right now (I'll wait).

Set the reminder for 9pm.

Done?

Now, for the next month (yes, a month, it takes 1 minute per day, you can do it), each night write down 3 things for which you are grateful. They can be little things (like, I went to do my nails and they look gorgeous) or big things (OMG, he just proposed!!!). But you really have to focus on them and actually formulate them – just a word or a short phrase. And as you write these things down, take a moment to be mindful of the things you're writing about. *Feel the gratitude.* And then see your happiness levels steadily climb.

I've been doing it for almost a year, every single day. Thanks to technology, I don't have to rely on my memory, which definitely helps. Believe me, it makes a huge difference. Start doing it *today*.

6. Helping others

> "If you want happiness for an hour, take a nap.
> If you want happiness for a day, go fishing.
> If you want happiness for a year, inherit a fortune.
> If you want happiness for a lifetime, help someone else."
> *Chinese Proverb*

So... This may blow your mind but... unlike it may seem at first glance, **doing good things for others is actually a selfish act.** Yep. Simply because for any normal human being, helping someone generates good feelings. On top of that, it can also increase our feelings of social connection.

In 2006, a group of scientists[28] examined the relationship between the character strength of kindness and subjective happiness. They found that simply counting one's own acts of kindness for one week increased subjective happiness. Moreover, merely *thinking* about acts of kindness makes you feel happier.

Let's all now agree that the "selfish" nature of kind acts doesn't make them less honorable. Others benefit and you become a happier person. What's not to like???

If you think about it, in most cases it really doesn't take much to help another person in a difficult situation. Normally it's one of the two: time or money. Neither of the above is more important than being a decent human being, and a happy one.

I have to note here (important!) that **by no means should helping others come with a sacrifice to yourself.** This should *never*

---

[28] Keiko Otake et al, "Happy People Become Happier through Kindness: A Counting Kindnesses Intervention" (2006)

happen. Never do anything that would hurt you. Never sacrifice or allow others to take advantage of you.

There's a difference between doing things for others while hurting yourself and sacrificing your own happiness, vs doing things for others because you actually enjoy it. If you sacrifice yourself for others, you will quickly find yourself being exploited as others begin to take advantage of you. And they will, not because they're bad but because you let them... #beentheredonethat. But if you can help another person without taking away from your own happiness – do it, don't think twice.

When you do good things as a result of an informed, reasonable decision, and that adds to the happiness of others as well as yourself, then you will not have a problem with saying "No" when your own inner peace is at risk. So, you won't allow others to take advantage of you. Huge difference!

I'll provide an example, for context.

Recently, I hosted a family of refugees from Ukraine, a mother and a daughter who ran from the war. I had never met them before, we connected through friends and I discovered that they were looking for shelter in San Diego where I live. I had a couple spare bedrooms in my house so I offered them free housing. It didn't cost me much, I didn't sacrifice anything, so I said yes. Needless to say, it changed their lives. But what is fascinating is that every day while they were living with me and I was doing little things to help them establish themselves in the new country away from home, I felt absolutely ecstatic. I had "my Ukrainian guests" as one of the things I was grateful for in my gratitude journal *every single day* during that time because I was happy to see my efforts materialize into little successes, one by one. They quickly found jobs and moved to a new house. We're now good friends and they're very grateful. Positive vibes all around.

6. Helping others

Compare this to the following. A few weeks later, another Ukrainian refugee reached out to me. She started with "Help me!" and then sent me 10 (!) voice messages, sobbing, describing her abusive relationship with her boyfriend, how she needs to run away from him, how she doesn't have any money and how badly she needs a free place to stay. Later I discovered that her boyfriend wasn't physically abusive, he was just mean. I was like: "Girl, welcome to the club!" I know many women who are in miserable relationships but they're not running around screaming. When I was in one, I was dealing with it myself, nobody knew. I mean, of course it's not healthy to be in an unhappy relationship and it's okay to ask for help. But there are different ways to do that.

I felt bad for her but honestly, I had no desire to help. First of all, the whole story had "drama" stamped all over it. And this drama was generated by that lady who just clearly enjoyed being a victim. She needed a therapist, not me. Secondly, I didn't know what her boyfriend was capable of, so I didn't want to put my children at risk. If I was in a state of a victim myself, ready to let anyone take advantage of me (which, by the way, I have absolutely done in the past on multiple occasions) I would have offered her to move in with me, thus saturating my household with drama for many months. But because I've learned to prioritize my mental health over anything else (one of the main elements of becoming an eternally happy human being), I said no. And I didn't feel guilty about it for even a split second.

Some might judge me for that decision. And they may have the right to do so. But that won't affect what I think about myself. Because remember, not being dependent on other people's opinion is another crucial element of being a self-sufficient, self-accepting, happy human being.

I've been criticized for helping others too much. True story. It didn't make me stop helping though. It made me start hiding my good deeds from judgmental people. Like smuggling $10,000 into Belarus, my home country, to give to my former ski coach, who played a huge role in shaping my personality and thus, my life. 10 k is about as much as an average Belarusian makes in a year, so you can imagine how this affected him and his family. Though it probably affected me more. I couldn't sleep, I was so excited.

Throughout my life, I've done some crazy stuff for others that most people wouldn't do. But I will never regret it because every time I did that, I became a happier person.

There's another benefit: it teaches you to appreciate what others do for you. #gratitude

Ungrateful people are those who are not used to helping others. Well, they're missing out. Because **giving is much more enjoyable than receiving.**

● EXERCISE

DO THIS EVERY DAY FOR A WEEK:

Random Acts of Kindness

This is from "Pathway to happiness program"[29] developed by the University of Berkeley.

---

[29] University of Berkeley, Greater Good in Action: Random Acts of Kindness (2022): https://ggia.berkeley.edu/practice/random_acts_of_kindness

6. Helping others

Research shows that happy people are motivated to do kind things for others. Over the next seven days, perform seven acts of kindness beyond what you normally do. You can do one extra act of kindness per day, or you can do a few acts of kindness in a single day.

It could be something major like donating money or volunteering in your community. Or it can be small, but something that really helps or impacts another person. For example, help your colleague with something, give a few dollars or some time to a cause you believe in, say something kind to a stranger, write a thank you note, give blood, and so on.

At the end of each day, list your random act of kindness. You can make a list in a notebook, keep a running note on your phone, log in a daily planner, or whatever method works for you. Just make sure you've finished seven total new acts of kindness by the end of the week. Beware: *this will change your life.*

7. Taking care of your body

> "A vigorous five-mile walk will do more good
> for an unhappy but otherwise healthy adult
> than all the medicine and psychology in the world."
> *Paul Dudley White*

For some reason, many people underestimate the importance of taking care of your body if your goal is to have a healthy mind. And I assume you'd like to have a healthy mind (unless you're my ex or the current president of Russia). There goes the Russian portion of my readers...

Anyway...

As mentioned earlier, emotions don't just happen in our head. Emotions represent the brain-body connection. And what happens in our body (a whole range of biological events) has a very significant impact on our mood. So we want our bodies to be healthy in order to be able to process our emotions in a healthier way.

There are three very important things that you can do to *help your body help you*: exercising regularly, sleeping well and eating healthy.

PHYSICAL ACTIVITY

For the purpose of our discussion, it's important to understand that in addition to helping your body just be healthier overall, **exercise boosts dopamine and helps your energy levels and overall mental condition.**

As you may or may not be aware, it's been scientifically proven that there's a whole host of benefits associated with physical activity that are related to your mind, not just your body. Exercise positively affects your mood. In fact, it can *decrease depression symptoms as much as an anti-depression medication like Zoloft.* For individuals with major depressive disorders, exercise therapy is feasible and is associated with significant therapeutic benefits, especially if exercise is continued over time.[30] It can also increase your academic and professional performance.

What's cool is that you don't have to become a professional athlete to start reaping the rewards. You just need to be a bit more active. For example, I find it enough to **perform some type of physical activity at least 3 times a week for at least 30 minutes.** I do yoga on Monday, I jog on Wednesday and I play volleyball on Saturday. You can hit the gym or take a fast-paced walk – whatever works for you. The key is to make sure it's *consistent.* And *track your activity* so you can develop a long-term habit (there's an app for that).

Free advice: adding exercise to your weekly calendar works best. This way, you won't forget, and, more importantly, you'll feel more obligated to commit to it since you've already allocated time for this activity in your busy schedule (as you should, because remember, we've already learned to prioritize ourselves over anything else). If you do this for a month, you'll notice how this will become an addiction and you won't be able to imagine your life without it (needless to say, this addiction is somewhat healthier than some others). No reminders will be needed. And you'll end up becoming happier and healthier.

---

[30] M Babyak et al, "Exercise treatment for major depression: maintenance of therapeutic benefit at 10 months" (2000)

7. Taking care of your body

What I also find helpful is making sure to notice how much better you feel after the exercise. *Savor it,* immerse in it. It's an amazing feeling when your legs (or any other body parts) are so sore that you can hardly walk. Wouldn't you agree? The feeling of accomplishment that comes with it is also priceless. Exercise is the best and the healthiest way to get that healing dopamine boost, which is what makes it addictive if you turn it into a consistent routine.

SLEEP

One of the reasons why so many people are unhappy in our modern society is that many are constantly sleep deprived. **Research shows that sleep improves your mood more than we often expect.**

Science proves that making sure you get enough sleep increases your mood over time.[31] It can also increase your cognitive performance, decrease your risk of heart disease, diabetes and even cancer. What's great about it is that it's totally free and super easy.

Try to shoot for around *7 to 8 hours a night.* Another life hack for you – start *tracking your sleep.* There are multiple mobile apps available for that. Just like with exercise, tracking it helps turn getting a healthy amount of sleep into a habit.

Proper sleep patterns make us happier. Period. That should be a good enough reason to start working on improving your sleep patterns *today.*

---

[31] D F Dinges et al, "Cumulative sleepiness, mood disturbance, and psychomotor vigilance performance decrements during a week of sleep restricted to 4-5 hours per night" (1997)

But if the above is not convincing enough, here's this:

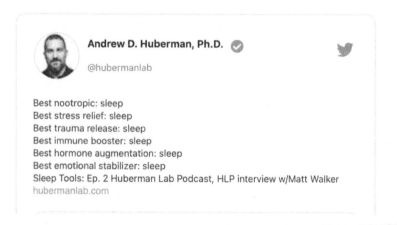

More on this can be found in Episode 2 "Master Your Sleep"[32] of the Huberman Lab Podcast by Andrew Huberman, the Stanford professor of neuroscience.

What I also found interesting is that consistency in your sleep matters more than just the amount of hours you sleep. You can also get more details on that in the above-mentioned podcast episode. Meaning that if you fall asleep around the same time and wake up around the same time every day, this will have a more positive effect on your overall mental and physical state than sleeping a sufficient amount of hours every day but on a random schedule.

To conclude, here's more from my favorite scientist: "Sleep is THE foundation of our mental and physical health and performance in all endeavors. Yet no one is perfect about sleep. The occasional night out or missing sunlight viewing here and there is not a big deal, so don't obsess over that. However, if any of us drift from these and the other behaviors for too long, we start to suffer. So

---

[32] Huberman Lab: Master Your Sleep and Be Alert When Awake (January 2021): https://hubermanlab.com/master-your-sleep-and-be-more-alert-when-awake/

whatever your life and goals and schedule, master your sleep. You'll be so happy you did!"[33] (Andrew D. Huberman)

FOOD

The podcast episode from Andrew Huberman entitled "How Foods and Nutrients Control our Moods"[34] contains a wealth of information backed by the latest scientific research on how specific foods we eat can affect our moods and motivation through dopamine and serotonin release in the brain. During that episode, Dr. Huberman discusses omega-3 fatty acids and the role of the gut microbiome in supporting or hindering mental and emotional wellbeing.

We are indeed what we eat.

Of course it goes without saying that you should be considerate to your body and develop healthy eating habits. You've heard this a gazillion times in your life but I'll say it again: eat a variety of vegetables, fruits, whole-grain, high-fiber breads and cereals, reduce or eliminate refined or processed carbohydrates, choose from a variety of low-fat sources of protein, reduce intake of saturated fats and trans-fats as well as the daily intake of salt or sodium, restrict or eliminate sodas and other sugar-added drinks that are high in calories and contain few or no nutrients and stay away from alcoholic and highly caffeinated beverages. This will help you sustain your physical health.

But what's also interesting is that what we eat really matters in terms of the neuro-chemicals that we make, which ultimately affect our mood.

---

[33] Huberman Lab: Toolkit For Sleep (September 2021): https://hubermanlab.com/toolkit-for-sleep/

[34] Huberman Lab: How Foods and Nutrients Control Our Moods (March 2021): (https://hubermanlab.com/how-foods-and-nutrients-control-our-moods/

For example, most people don't know the simple fact that the Omega-3 to Omega-6 fatty acid ratio has a profound effect on depression and mood. Recent findings[35] show that consuming 1,000 mg of EPA daily over the course of 8 weeks is *equally effective as Prozac* in reducing depressive symptoms. What's also notable is that the effect of antidepressants is *enhanced* with the consumption of EPA. EPA is one of the elements that contains high levels of Omega-3. It's present in fish oil among other things. So if you'd like some more help with boosting your mood – consider taking fish oil as a supplement (make sure it contains 1000 mg of EPA). Keep in mind there are side effects associated with fish oil, so just like with any supplements – make sure to check with your doctor first. But the effects of EPA on mood are really profound.

Regardless of whether you decide to start taking supplements, it's always a good idea to stick to healthy eating habits.

Long story short: **take care of your body and it will help you take care of your mind.**

• EXERCISE (LITERALLY)

DO THIS TODAY:

1. Install an app for tracking your physical activity

2. Install an app for tracking your sleep

---

[35] Shima Jazayeri et al, "Comparison of Therapeutic Effects of Omega-3 Fatty Acid Eicosapentaenoic Acid and Fluoxetine, Separately and in Combination, in Major Depressive Disorder" (2008)

3. If you need an additional mood boost – ask your doctor if it's safe for you to take fish oil (1000 mg EPA) as a supplement

DO THIS EVERY DAY FOR A MONTH:

Regular physical activity

When planning your weekly schedule, set aside a specific time for at least 30 minutes of exercise daily, or every other day at minimum. Plan the location and the type of exercise in advance.

Hit the gym, take a yoga class (even an online class will do), or throw on some headphones and get out for a run. This isn't supposed to be a marathon-level of activity; it's just to get your body moving a bit more than usual.

Be sure to take a moment to notice how much better you feel after getting some exercise in. Make a mental note of this feeling of accomplishment and sore muscles, savor it. Enjoy the sore butt! This will make it easier to get off that butt and do it again the next day.

Make sure to log your activity. Track your exercise until you become a complete addict (or at least for a month) and watch your mood magically improve, day after day.

Regular healthy sleep

This is from Andrew Huberman's Sleep Toolkit.[36] Here's what Professor Huberman suggests to implement in order to improve

---

[36] Huberman Lab: Toolkit For Sleep (September 2021): https://hubermanlab. com/toolkit-for-sleep/

your sleep habits. All suggestions are based on prior scientific studies. This is absolutely invaluable information. Pure gold. By making these things a habit, many aspects of your life will improve, including your mood. Proven by science. Confirmed by yours truly.

1. View sunlight by going outside within 30-60 minutes of waking. Do that again in the late afternoon, prior to sunset. Don't wear sunglasses for this practice if you safely can, but contact lenses and eyeglasses are fine. No, you don't have to look directly at the sun.

2. *Wake up at the same time each day and go to sleep when you first start to feel sleepy.* Pushing through the sleepy late evening feeling and going to sleep too late (for you) is one reason people wake at 3 am and can't fall back asleep.

3. Avoid caffeine within 8-10 hours of bedtime.

4. If you have sleep disturbances, insomnia, or anxiety about sleep, try the research-supported protocols on the Reveri mobile app. Do the Reveri sleep self-hypnosis 3x a week at any time of day. It's only 10-15 min long and will help you rewire your nervous system to be able to relax faster.

5. Avoid viewing bright lights – especially bright overhead lights between 10 pm and 4 am. *Yes, that includes your cell phone.*

6. Limit daytime naps to less than 90 min, or don't nap at all.

7. If you wake up in the middle of the night (which, by the way, is normal) but you can't fall back asleep, consider

doing an NSDR protocol. Enter "NSDR" into YouTube and the top 3-4 options have different voices, durations for you to select from. Or simply do a "Yoga Nidra" protocol (enter "yoga nidra" to YouTube; 100^s to select from).

8. Keep the room you sleep in cool and dark and layer on blankets that you can remove. Your body needs to drop in temperature by 1-3 degrees to fall and stay asleep effectively. Body temperature increases are one reason you wake up.

9. Drinking alcohol messes up your sleep. As do most sleep medications.

8. Learning to be present

*"A human mind is a wandering mind,
and a wandering mind is an unhappy mind,"*
Matthew A. Killingsworth and Daniel T. Gilbert, Journal Science

Based on one of the studies conducted by Harvard psychologists, people spend 46.9 percent of their waking hours *thinking about something other than what they're doing*. We're having dinner with our friends but thinking about that report we forgot to submit to our boss. We're playing with our kids but in our heads we're actually planning our week and all the errands we need to run. We're spending a romantic evening with a loved one but our mind is calculating the amount of tax we owe to the government. We're walking in the park where beautiful leaves are dancing together as they fall gradually on the ground near our feet but in our heads we're replaying that conversation from last night where we said what we shouldn't have or we didn't say what we should have. We allow days filled with happy joyful moments go by unnoticed because we live in our own heads or in our phones instead of living in the present and interacting with the world around us. As a result, this **"mind-wandering" makes us unhappy,** which has recently been proven by scientists.[37]

And that's because happiness lies not in the big things that we dream about (like a higher salary or a new house). It's in the little things that we miss if we're not paying attention. **Happiness lies in noticing little moments that give you joy. And the more you notice them, the more you register them, the more you remember them – the happier you are.**

---

[37] Harvard University: Wandering mind not a happy mind (2010): https://news.harvard.edu/gazette/story/2010/11/wandering-mind-not-a-happy-mind/

Why are we doing so much "wandering"? Turns out there's such a thing as "default network"[38] in our brain that is activated when a person is not involved in a task, not concentrating on something specific. It comes on within a fraction of a second after a task is completed. That's what our minds do when we get out of "here and now".

But even when we're performing an activity, 30 percent of the time we're still mind-wandering. That pertains to all activities except for... ready? Except for sex. At least we're fully present when we reproduce... Which is probably the ultimate reason why we're still not extinct.

Where was I...

Yes. Scientists proved[39] that mind-wandering has a negative impact on happiness. Daniel Gilbert, one of the co-authors of that study, points out that "the ability to think about what is not happening is a cognitive achievement that comes at an emotional cost."

So what can we do to stop our minds from wandering and become happy humans?

It's actually not that hard but it takes practice. **You need to train your brain to be in the moment, to be present.** Tools in this chapter will help you with that. Needless to say, learning to meditate helps a lot as well but that meaningful practice deserves its own dedicated chapter, which you will find further in this book.

---

[38] Matthew A. Killingsworth and Daniel T. Gilbert, "A Wandering Mind Is an Unhappy Mind" (2010)

[39] Matthew A. Killingsworth and Daniel T. Gilbert, "A Wandering Mind Is an Unhappy Mind" (2010)

8. Learning to be present

In our modern society with our busy lives, we tend to constantly disconnect from our reality. We tend to run from one task to another, not paying our full attention to things around us or truly enjoying them. But what you will hopefully soon realize is, **true happiness lies in those little moments when you actually stop running and are fully present.** Train your brain to recognize them. It's not that hard. And once you master it, teach your friends to do the same. You'll make them happier, too. And they'll be grateful.

Moral of the story: **Put down your phone, Instagram will wait. Be present. Learn to enjoy the little things.**

● EXERCISES

DO THIS EVERY DAY FOR A WEEK:

Mental screenshot practice

Here's one way to train your brain to truly register joyful moments, which ultimately helps you build up the "happiness baseline". As you pay more attention to these moments, the more of them you'll remember, and the healthier your overall mindset will be.

This is how it goes and it's very easy and actually fun. Whenever you catch yourself smiling about something or enjoying an event or somebody's presence, in other words, if you feel happy or joyful or just peaceful (and believe me, those moments happen to you on a daily basis, regardless of your life circumstances, you just need to start noticing them) – stop for a second, immerse yourself fully in this moment, bathe in this feeling, then close your eyes and pretend you're taking a "snapshot" of what you're seeing and feeling, and "add it to your memory bank".

When you're having dinner with your friends, look at them, smile, feel how thankful you are that you have them in your life. Take a snapshot. When playing with your kids, stop, look at them with love, feel the joy of the moment when they run around happily screaming. Take a snapshot. When walking in the park, breathe in the fresh air, thank yourself for the ability to get out and just walk, some people don't have that. Take a snapshot. When having a romantic evening with your loved one, put your phone down, be present, cuddle, talk. Take a snapshot. When having sex... you know, keep doing what you're doing.

So, by engaging your full concentration on the present moment, this technique encourages the formation and accumulation of joyful memories and scenes that otherwise go unnoticed and tend to get lost in the chaos of our daily thoughts. How it works is this: the more of these "snapshots" you gather over time, the higher your perception of your quality of life is, so you start considering yourself a happier person. You're not "tricking" your brain into believing that you actually have a happy life. You just help your brain recognize that it's ultimately true and that your life is full of joyful moments because you have learned to start noticing them.

Aside from teaching you how to be present, if you practice this habit, it steadily raises your happiness baseline, which then helps you deal with other things in your life in a more controlled, healthy way.

Savoring

This is taken from Laurie Santos' course "The Science of Well-Being" offered by Yale University on Coursera.[40] I found it extremely effective. It has a lot of overlap with the "mental screenshot"

---

[40] Coursera: The Science of Well-Being by Laurie Santos (offered by Yale): https://www.coursera.org/learn/the-science-of-well-being

technique, although it's a bit different, so you can pick either one to practice throughout the following week.

First off, what is savoring? It's just the simple act of stepping out of your experience, to review it, and really appreciating it while it's happening. As we discussed above, often we fail to stay in the moment and really enjoy what we're experiencing. Savoring intensifies and lengthens the positive emotions that come with doing something you love.

Why should we take time to savor? It turns out savoring can boost our mood in at least three ways. First, savoring can thwart hedonic adaptation, which is getting used to things that previously made us happy but no longer do. It can make us remember and keep enjoying the good stuff in life. Second, savoring can help thwart mind wandering. It keeps us in the moment. And finally, savoring can help us increase gratitude. It can make us thankful for the experiences we're having as we're having them.

For the next seven days, practice the art of savoring by picking one experience to truly savor each day. It could be a nice shower, a delicious meal, a great walk outside, or any experience that you really enjoy. Hint: you can pick one from your "things that give you energy and make you happy" list that you put together when reading the "Sorting your life" chapter. When you take part in this savored experience, be sure to practice some common techniques that enhance savoring. First, take a second to realize why it makes you happy. Other techniques include: sharing the experience with another person, thinking about how lucky you are to enjoy such an amazing moment, keeping a souvenir or photo of that activity, and making sure you stay in the present moment the entire time. Every night, make a note of what you savored. When you do write things down at the end of the day, be sure to take a moment to remember the activity.

So get out there and savor something good. Go out and really enjoy the best things in life.

9. Meditation

"You should sit in meditation for 20 minutes a day,
unless you're too busy, then you should sit for an hour."
Zen Proverb

I wasn't a believer in the power of meditation until I became desperate enough to try it. I was in a pretty bad stage of my life and was just trying everything that I could think of, so I figured "why not, things can't get worse than they already are". And should I say, I was in for a surprise. After mastering it for a few months, I remember the day when I sat in complete stillness for about 40 minutes with an absolutely empty head (what a relief it was) and my soul flying somewhere outside of my body. I could clearly feel that. It was the most unforgettable state of complete serenity, worth living and dying for. I had never experienced anything like that before, and I probably wouldn't have if I hadn't started meditating.

If you are unfamiliar with this wonderful tool, meditation is a practice in which an individual uses a technique – such as mindfulness, or focusing the mind on a particular object, thought, or activity – to train attention and awareness, and achieve a mentally clear and emotionally calm and stable state.[41] Essentially what you do is teach your "monkey brain" to concentrate on a single point of reference (most often it is the breathing or sometimes it can be some other specific sensation in your body) instead of swinging from one branch (thought) to another.

Positive effects of meditation have been proven again and again, yet there are still many people who have never attempted

---

[41] Wikipedia: Mediation: https://en.wikipedia.org/wiki/Meditation

to meditate. I absolutely encourage you to try it as soon as you finish reading this chapter. You'll do yourself a huge favor and you'll move one step closer to becoming an ultimately serene and happy individual. With that, you'll also make me happy because I'll feel good about myself for changing your life forever.

One of the studies[42] confirmed that meditators shut off the "default network" that we spoke about in the previous chapter. In other words – their minds wander less, which ultimately affects their mood and their quality of life in general. It's interesting to note that for people who practice meditation consistently, the effect also spreads outside of the actual meditation activity, changing their default behavior throughout the day. This allows them to focus more and learn to be present in their daily lives (which leads to an increase in happiness, as we now know).

There are numerous other studies that have shown additional benefits from meditation practice: generating positive emotions[43], stress reduction[44], boosting cognitive performance[45], and even increasing the size of your brain matter and strengthening your brain[46].

---

[42] Judson A. Brewer et al, "Meditation experience is associated with differences in default mode network activity and connectivity" (2011)

[43] Barbara L. Fredrickson et al, "Open Hearts Build Lives: Positive Emotions, Induced Through Loving-Kindness Meditation, Build Consequential Personal Resources" (2011)

[44] Britta K. Hölzel et al, "How Does Mindfulness Meditation Work? Proposing Mechanisms of Action From a Conceptual and Neural Perspective" (2011)

[45] Michael D Mrazek et al, "Mindfulness training improves working memory capacity and GRE performance while reducing mind wandering" (2013)

[46] Harvard University: Meditation found to increase brain size (2006): https://news.harvard.edu/gazette/story/2006/02/meditation-found-to-increase-brain-size/

If you're still not convinced, here's more: in addition to balancing your mental and emotional health, meditation calms your brain and body, it teaches you to breathe better, it helps you soothe pain, it improves your concentration and sleep. Again, what's not to like! #no-brainer

Treat it like hygiene for your brain and for your soul. You have learned to keep your body clean, you take a shower on a daily basis, right? Well, at least I hope you do... So in the same manner, we need to get used to keeping our minds clean as well.

So try it out today. Meditate for 10 minutes. And hopefully, you will make it a habit, a very healthy, life-changing habit.

● EXERCISE

DO THIS EVERY DAY, FOR A WEEK:

Guided meditation

Install an app. I personally use "Calm" but there are a few other ones that are as awesome: Headspace, Insight Timer, etc. Many of them offer a free basic subscription with the option to upgrade to a premium version that offers more features. If you're a beginner, use recorded guided meditations that are available in the app. I still do that, even though I've been meditating for years. There's something very attractive about being able to delegate all the thinking to another person. :)

For the next week, spend at least 10 minutes per day meditating. You can keep increasing the time as you get more practice, but for now 10 minutes will suffice. Try to do it at the same time of the day, which will increase your chances of making it a habit.

Find a quiet spot where you won't be disturbed while you're meditating. It may seem weird or hard at first. Also, if you're sleep deprived, don't be surprised if you doze off, that's fine, though that should tell you that you might want to rethink your sleeping patterns. The key is to not worry about how well you're doing. Just relax and follow the voice. As you keep practicing it daily, you will notice how much calmer you become. You will also notice how much clearer your head is and one day you'll be able to reach those states of complete serenity without any effort.

10. Therapy and Psychedelics

*"You live in a limitless reality.
Whatever boundary you construct is a lingering
self-created thought.
There is a paradise beyond."
Vladimir Hlocky, Journeys Beyond Earth*

If you have been practicing the concepts and tools offered in this book for at least some time, I'm sure you're already noticing the difference and finding yourself to be a whole new, happier human. You may not even recognize yourself (told ya!).

But if you have childhood traumas that are hidden deep in the subconscious levels of your psyche, especially if you've been suppressing a lot throughout your life, or if you consider yourself chronically depressed, there might be a need to resort to more invasive tools to dig those deeper things out of your head.

With the help of those tools, you can literally 'un-traumatize' yourself (I think I just invented a new word). Yes, it's absolutely possible. As they say, it's never too late to have a happy childhood.

The tools I'm referring to may be either hypnotic therapy or psychedelic drugs. I've tried both (there goes another portion of my readers) and I would say they're equally effective.

So, hypnosis. **Cognitive behavioral hypnotherapy (CBH)** is an integrated psychological therapy employing clinical hypnosis and cognitive behavioral therapy (CBT). The use of CBT together with hypnotherapy results in greater treatment effectiveness. An analysis of eight different researches revealed a 70 percent greater improvement for patients undergoing an integrated treatment to those using CBT only.[47]

When I was in a very (very-very) crappy mental condition, my therapist resurrected me in one 2-hour session with the help of hypnosis. It wasn't easy, I was thrown back into my childhood, I was crying, drooling, I faced some major fears and traumas, I was more miserable than ever. At the end of the session, she carefully pulled me out of it and I felt like I was born again. I got up the next day and moved on with my life, smiling, like none of that happened. And the session was held over Skype. I'm not kidding.

So if you think you have a lot of baggage – definitely keep practicing the tools you just learned from the previous pages that will help consistently build up your "happiness baseline", which is essential, but consider looking for a CBH therapist. There IS hope, I promise. You can, and absolutely will, live a light, happy, joyful life. You just need to get that stuff out of your head. And it's okay to ask for help.

Now, the more exciting part of this discussion – **therapy with the help of psychedelics.**

The readers who were looking for a magic pill and dropped off after the second chapter – please return.

Needless to say, I can NOT recommend taking any types of drugs, even legal ones. You have to make that decision yourself, I wouldn't take that responsibility. Please do a thorough research before taking anything that is not prescribed by your doctor. Talk to

---

[47] I Kirsch et al, "Hypnosis as an adjunct to cognitive-behavioral psychotherapy: a meta-analysis" (1995)

your therapist, read about it, familiarize yourself with side effects and make sure it's a conscious decision of a mature adult.

Okay, now that we're done with the disclaimer, I will proceed. As much as I don't want you to treat this chapter as a recommendation, I also can't NOT talk about psychedelics here because of their increasing role in therapy in modern society and in my personal life in particular. There's a reason why a psychedelic session is consistently referred to as "10 years of therapy in one night"... though in my case it was more like 20.

What is considered a psychedelic drug? Psychedelics are a class of hallucinogenic drugs whose primary effect is to trigger non-ordinary states of consciousness, known as psychedelic experiences or "trips". This causes specific psychological, visual, and auditory changes, and often a substantially altered state of consciousness. The "classical" psychedelics, the ones with the largest scientific and cultural influence, are mescaline, LSD, psilocybin, and DMT.[48]

According to the National Library of Medicine, psychedelics are generally considered physiologically safe and do not lead to dependence or addiction.[49]

Note that psilocybin (found in so-called "magic mushrooms") is now legal in many US states. The movement to decriminalize psilocybin in our country began in the late 2010s, with Denver, Colorado becoming the first city to decriminalize it in May 2019.[50]

---

[48] Wikipedia: Psychedelic drug: https://en.wikipedia.org/wiki/Psychedelic_drug

[49] David E. Nichols, "Psychedelics" (2016)

[50] Wikipedia: Psilocybin decriminalization in the United States: https://en.wikipedia.org/wiki/Psilocybin_decriminalization_in_the_United_States

In 2020, the US Government funded the first therapeutic psilocybin research in 50 Years.[51]

As of this writing (Summer 2022), LSD and MDMA are still considered illegal drugs in the US and so is DMT, which is found in Ayahuasca for example. Ayahuasca is legal in Mexico, Peru and some other countries in South America.[52]

Fun fact. Founder of AA (Alcoholic Anonymous) Bill Wilson used psychedelic drug (LSD in particular) to finally get past his desperately severe alcoholism. Wilson is known to have taken LSD in supervised experiments in the 1950s with Betty Eisner, an American psychologist known for pioneering the use of LSD and other psychedelic drugs. "I am certain that the LSD experiment has helped me very much," Wilson wrote in a 1957 letter. "I find myself with a heightened color perception and an appreciation of beauty almost destroyed by my years of depression."[53] Don Lattin, an American journalist, wrote about Wilson's experience with psychedelics in his book "Distilled Spirits"[54](2012).

Matthew Johnson, Ph.D Professor at Johns Hopkins, is on the forefront of the most recent research on psychedelics. In fact, you may have seen him on TV recently, he's been very vocal

[51] Rolling Stone: U.S. Government Funds First Therapeutic Psilocybin Research in 50 Years (2020): https://www.rollingstone.com/culture/culture-features/psychedelic-psilocybin-smoking-quit-study-federal-funding-1255524/

[52] Wikipedia: Legal status of ayahuasca by country: https://en.wikipedia.org/wiki/Legal_status_of_ayahuasca_by_country

[53] The Guardian: LSD could help alcoholics stop drinking, AA founder believed (2012): https://www.theguardian.com/science/2012/aug/23/lsd-help-alcoholics-theory#

[54] Don Lattin, "Distilled Spirits – Getting High, Then Sober, With a Famous Writer, a Forgotten Philosopher, and a Hopeless" (2012)

about his studies. He published the first research on psychedelic treatment of tobacco addiction in 2014, and the largest study of psilocybin in treating cancer-related depression and anxiety in 2016. To date, he has supervised the administration of over 600 psychedelic sessions.

As you may know, this isn't the first time psychedelics have been tested to treat mental health but research stopped in 1970 due to drug histeria even though the findings were very promising. It took a few decades for the histeria to blow over and for this research to be allowed again, finally, due to vast amounts of supporting data.

Dr. Johnson has conducted numerous studies and the results are incredible. **Psychedelic drugs can treat mental health disorders (PTSD, anxiety, chronic depression) as well as substance addiction.** After just one session, people often reframe and reprioritize what's going on in their lives. Issues that seemed insurmountable all of a sudden are trivialized. Smokers quit smoking. Cancer patients' lives stop being dominated by the obsessive thought of being doomed and they continue living a fulfilled life. Anxieties and fears go away.

As Johnson describes, a third of the patients on a high dose report something that may be called a "bad trip". However, most people would report that those difficult experiences during the psychedelic therapy session were the most meaningful and spiritually significant events they've had in their lives.

He is advocating for psychedelics to become a new field of medicine, a new paradigm in psychiatry, as meditation-facilitated psychotherapy. Keep in mind, **we're not talking about regular use of these drugs. Psychedelics don't *cause* addiction, they're used to *treat* it. A single session can have a long-lasting effect.** As we know, both addiction and depression are a big problem in our society, and both can be addressed if the FDA approves psychedelics for treating mental health.

Keep in mind that people in these studies at John Hopkins are carefully screened to eliminate psychiatric vulnerability: predisposition to psychotic disorders. So (again!) make sure to check with your therapist if you decide to try any of these substances.

A little bit about my personal experience with psychedelics. I've tried a few different types, and always – solely for therapeutic purposes (being able to watch cartoons with your eyes closed is not the main benefit of these substances, in my opinion). As mentioned earlier, classic psychedelic drugs are not known for causing addiction. I confirm. After one session – there's no desire to do it again for quite a while, especially if the "trip" was deep, strong and full of insights.

By far, the strongest experience I've had was during an Ayahuasca ceremony, which was held outside of the US. 20 years of therapy in one night, indeed. A few highlights: the shaman was "a real deal", a Peruvian who literally studied for 5 years in the Amazon to properly conduct these ceremonies. A big part of the ceremony is the atmosphere (mainly, the music and the actions of the shaman), not just the drug itself. Most of these are held at night, starting around 7-8 pm. The whole thing normally lasts 4-6 hours (that's how long it takes your body to process it), then many people go to sleep and wake up reborn. There are multiple stages in the process, one of which is called "purging". I'll refrain from describing the details here, you can look it up if interested. During the ceremony, some people go through "near-death" experiences (I did). I then cried my eyes out for 3 hours straight. I totally had what you would call a "bad trip" and at this point, a year later, I have zero desire to go through that again. Ever. But just like what Dr. Johnson was describing above: I am eternally grateful for this experience because it was *the most meaningful event of my life that healed my soul.*

I woke up the next morning feeling lighter than ever. On that same day, I wrote down all the insights I had that night. I remembered everything clearly, I still do. And I wrote a blog post that I'm sharing with you below. Even though all of those things may seem like common sense, I have to clarify that every single one of these insights is now a part of me, they're no longer just statements to me, they're not theory, they are the essence of my life. It's been a year since I participated in the ceremony and I still live by these principles.

Here it goes. Hope you find it inspirational. Many of my friends did when I shared it with them.

"What I learned when I was dying.

On June 5, 2021 I was born again. And I left my baggage in my previous life. Here's what I learned when I was dying.

- Life is a gift, use it to be a better version of yourself
- Find inner peace within yourself, it's in your heart
- Don't let your happiness be dependent on other people and circumstances
- Don't let guilt control your actions and your mind
- Don't take responsibility for other people's happiness, let them live their own lives
- Don't try to control everything, you can't; sometimes you just need to relax and let it go
- Sharing is good, don't hold everything inside
- Pain is inevitable but suffering is optional

- Be happy just because you are alive
- It's all up to us, we make the decision, we choose the life we want to live
- Past is past, let it go, it doesn't define you, live in the present
- Forgive
- Forgive from your heart, not your head
- Pain is always temporary, you will smile when it's over
- Appreciate your body, be grateful for what it is doing for you
- Don't try to explain everything rationally, sometimes you just need to believe
- Money is just money
- Meaningful connections matter. A lot.
- People don't only use words for communication, they exchange energy
- Stop judging, appreciate people for who they are
- Say what you mean, don't hold back
- Embrace your feminine energy, regardless of your gender
- You are great, you are enough, you have strength, you are important no matter what others think about you
- Smile
- Smile again
- And again
- Everything is going to be alright
- Enjoy every moment of your life, it's a precious gift"

As you may have guessed, these principles laid the foundation for this book. It took some time to sort through all the knowledge accumulated in my head over the last few years and put it on paper, but here I admit: if not for my experiences that night, this book would never have been born.

Aside from these insights that completely rebuilt my internal framework and helped me get rid of my baggage, another extremely valuable aspect of the experience was a crystal clear understanding of what had been making me unhappy. I was amazed that I didn't realize those things before. I find it shocking how hard it is for us, modern human beings, to be honest with ourselves. Often we live our lives depressed but not understanding what exactly is causing it. And sometimes you need to dig really deep to get to the root of the problem. With this understanding in mind, when I returned home after the ceremony, I made a few drastic changes in my life without hesitation (though I must admit, it wasn't easy), which allowed me to truly spread my wings, in many aspects.

I quit my job, which allowed me to start making money much easier with less hours and more joy. I built many new meaningful connections. I published a new book. I fell in love. I started teaching. And finally, I wrote the book you're holding in your hands, which I would call the culmination of my transformational journey. And hopefully yours, too.

● EXERCISE

If you're expecting my blessing for you to go do drugs – that ain't happening! Use your brain, talk to your therapist (if you have one), make your choice. If you don't think you're ready – don't do it. Or consider hypnotherapy. If you're not ready for that either – that means you're not desperate enough and you don't need it, great! Just continue practicing the tools from this book. You'll be in the state of eternal bliss in no time.

Please also note that the "invasive" tools mentioned in this chapter, while highly effective in many cases, cannot substitute the daily tools that are described throughout this book. Even if you go through deep transformations and become enlightened with the help of hypnosis or psychedelics – you need a way to sustain it and keep your mental core strong and your baseline elevated at the consistent level. Just like you need PT after having a surgery.

Bonus: Live your life, don't just exist

"Having fun is not a diversion from a successful life;
it is the pathway to it."
Martha Beck

This is probably my favorite chapter (though the previous one was fun, too, right?). It is less practical and more philosophical. It is not about any specific behavior or a habit. It is about the concept of living a meaningful, joyful life instead of simply existing.

What does it mean to live your life to the fullest? Well, it may mean many things to many people. But the key is **to do things that you actually enjoy doing, to have fun, on a large scale, rather than living your life doing things that you feel like you *have to* do for whatever reason.** And I don't mean just doing a few things here and there that you enjoy (which is a great first step towards happiness, as we discussed in one of the previous chapters) but ultimately living your entire life like that. *Yes, it IS possible!*

Now, this will require you to get rid of a few stereotypes. First one – that hedonism is bad and enjoying life is shameful. Second – that having fun won't get you too far if you want to be successful in life.

Let's just deal with those right now.

Do you want to be a happy person? Do you want to enjoy life? I do. I am. Many people are. Why wouldn't you allow yourself to do the same? *I am right now, as you're reading this sentence, allowing you to start enjoying life and not feel guilty about it. Because you deserve it. Because you were born with the right to be happy.*

Boom.

Ok. One down. Next.

Let's ask ourselves: what does it even mean, to be successful? You would probably say: "Making $X a year". Well, allow me to destroy this one. Multiple studies have confirmed that the *correlation between life satisfaction and income is very insignificant.*[55] In other words: contrary to many people's beliefs, if you make more money, you're not a happier person. You think your life is better, but not really.

One of the recent studies[56] has uncovered that people with an annual household income of $75,000 (this was in the US) are about as happy as anyone gets. With higher income comes flattened life satisfaction and happiness scores, and in many cases, the latter actually decline. As I can imagine, if you have to manage a multi-million dollar fortune, you probably have quite a few things to worry about on a daily basis.

In other words, once you have enough money to cover your basic needs, your financial situation starts having a very negligible effect, if not negative, on your happiness levels. So if your household has reached that golden 75 k mark – you're good, you can allow yourself to relax. However, as you may have noticed, that's the opposite from what most people do, at least in our society. Once we hit 75 k – we immediately ask for more. And then more. And more. Because we're a *generation of materialistic consumerists*. Most of us sacrifice our peace of mind for the sake of reaching yet another financial goal. And that's very wrong, because that's not why you were brought to this life.

---

[55] Ed Diener et al, "The Relationship Between Income and Subjective Well-Being: Relative or Absolute?" (1992)

[56] Daniel Kahneman and Angus Deaton, "High income improves evaluation of life but not emotional well-being" (2010)

Bonus: Live your life, don't just exist

By the way, I have no idea why exactly you were brought here, but I know for sure that it's not to work your butt off in that corner office with no windows. And I know that you understand that as well.

So back to our pursuit of happiness. Life is not about material things. Money is just money (you may recognize one of the insights I shared with you in the previous chapter; little did I know that this had been scientifically proven). *Money won't buy you happiness*, at least not in the long run, due to this phenomenon that scientists call "hedonic adaptation", which I mentioned earlier. Life is about doing things you actually enjoy. You have probably heard the phrase "Find a job you enjoy doing, and you will never have to work a day in your life". It's true. Have fun with your life and you'll be able to turn making money into a hobby while actually enjoying the process rather than hating your life if you hate what you do on a daily basis. **And yes, it is possible to have fun while making money and actually be a happy person.** I personally know quite a few people who live their lives this way, and I'm one of them. Those people are also perceived as "financially successful" because it's actually easier to make money if you love what you do, though wealth is normally not their main goal. Their main goal is to do things they enjoy doing.

On another note. Science confirms[57] that experiences matter more than material things and contribute more to our happiness. Experiential purchases (money spent on doing) tend to provide more enduring happiness than material purchases (money spent on having).[58] Materialists have much lower life satisfaction scores and more mental health disorders[59] (so much for that American

---

[57] Van Boven et al, "To Do or to Have? That Is the Question." (2003)

[58] Amit Kumar et al, "Waiting for Merlot: Anticipatory Consumption of Experiential and Material Purchases" (2014)

[59] Carol Nickerson et al, "Zeroing in on the Dark Side of the American Dream A Closer Look at the Negative Consequences of the Goal for Financial Success" (2003)

dream). Of course, because they're constantly worried about a bigger paycheck, they're on the phone with their clients instead of taking mental snapshots of joyful moments when playing with their kids.

The key is that **hedonic adaptation doesn't apply to experiences.** We don't "get used" to them as we do to a new car or a new house that first looked so exciting but then turned into yet another cage that's just bigger and shinier. When it comes to experiences though, we keep enjoying them again and again and we keep being excited about them.

Those who follow me on Instagram can probably tell that I intuitively came to that conclusion a long time ago. "Ira, we can't keep up with you, you're everywhere and you're always doing something" – is the most popular phrase I hear from my followers. By the way, experiences are also less susceptible to social comparison. I never post about new material things I acquire, I hardly ever shop. My stories are about traveling, writing, spending time with my kids and exercising, as well as those small moments of joy, like sitting on your butt in the sand staring at the ocean, with a cup of latte in your hand. It's those experiences that make us happier – that's what I want to share with the world. Although... guilty, I did post a picture of my Tesla when I bought it. Arguably though, Tesla is not just a car, it's an experience.

Long story short, it's been proven again and again[60] that **you'll be generally happier if you invest in experiences more than if you invest in "stuff".** It goes without saying that the activities you need to engage in ideally should suit your values and interests and be enjoyable to you.

---

[60] Sonja Lyubomirsky and Kennon M. Sheldon, "Pursuing Happiness: The Architecture of Sustainable Change" (2005)

Bonus: Live your life, don't just exist

This leads us to another aspect of our discussion.

The fun part is that **what gives us the deepest feeling of true happiness and fulfillment is not sitting on the couch watching Netflix**. Contrary to what many people believe, it's not the passive pastime that you need to seek. I have to note here that if you're desperate for some "me time" and just being horizontal, like a log, for an hour without anyone bothering you – that means you're probably overworked and you should absolutely find time to do just that – allow yourself to be a log (see chapter "Sorting your life"). It's a necessary step to improving your life. But hopefully when, after reading this book, your life has been improved to the point that "me time" is a natural part of your existence and not a luxury – you'll be ready to get to the next level. And the next level is the opposite from being a log.

Here's why.

Have you ever experienced that state of mind when you are doing something so engaging that you skip lunch and forget to pee? If you have – **make it a goal to experience this every single day.**

Now, pay attention. It's normal and desirable to just do random things for the sake of the experience: traveling for example or jumping out of a plane with a parachute. But true happiness seekers should know that the secret is to occasionally, or regularly, find an activity you truly *enjoy*, which is *challenging* and requires a high level of *skill*.

This blissful state has been studied by scientists for a while. Laurie Santos at Yale calls it "flow". Andrew Huberman at Stanford calls it a "tunnel". Others call it "being in the zone". **It is the mental**

state in which a person performing an activity is fully immersed in a feeling of energized focus, full involvement, and enjoyment. This is the ultimate way of living a fulfilled, joyfull, happy life.

Based on my personal experience, this state is more addictive than sugar. It gives you the feeling of purpose and accomplishment. As I realized recently, I'm so addicted to it, that if I don't experience it for some time, I subconsciously start changing and re-adapting my life, so I can challenge myself and start "flowing" again. In my life this manifests itself in quitting a job, picking up a new hobby, learning how to do a headstand, or writing a book.

Writing is one of the things that absolutely does it for me. When working on my previous book, I once spent 6 hours straight behind my computer. When I finally lifted my head, I thanked God that the bathroom was not very far... "And you did that with no Adderall??" – a friend inquired. The beauty is that when you're "flowing", your brain develops all kinds of chemicals to keep you going. That's why it's so addictive. It's an unforgettable feeling that no drugs would produce (yes, even psychedelics).

Now, the main point is that: we should all have the right to experience such bliss at work, regardless of what we do. So if looking back at the last year of your daily work life, you realize that you haven't been able to reach that state – you're not in the right place.

"The best moments in our lives are not the passive, receptive, relaxing times. The best moments usually occur if a person's body or mind is stretched to its limits in a voluntary effort to accomplish something difficult and worthwhile."[61] – says a person with an unpronounceable last name (Mihaly Csikszentmihalyi).

---

[61] Positive Psychology: 8 Ways To Create Flow According to Mihaly Csikszentmihalyi (2021): https://positivepsychology.com/mihaly-csikszentmihalyi-father-of-flow/

Bonus: Live your life, don't just exist

Some of you may have read "Hero on a Mission"[62] where Donald Miller talks about a similar concept. By the way, I recommend this book to all my students at SDSU even though it has nothing to do with the subject that I teach. I do that because I know that this book will change their lives as it did mine. "Hero on a Mission" helped me find my meaning after I had been relentlessly searching for it for years.

Why are we talking about meaning? Because it's **easier to be happier if you have a reason to wake up every day.**

According to Miller (and now to me), the meaning of life is in the *movement*. "Meaning doesn't fulfill our deepest longings, those longings that are a common part of the human experience. Meaning does, however, serve as a pleasant distraction. **Meaning is experienced in motion.** Even Jesus said "Follow me" rather than "Figure me out." We've spent way too much time studying meaning and way too little time experiencing meaning. Meaning happens when we move."

Essentially, what he says is that meaning is in these ongoing experiences that allow you to find yourself in the state of "flowing" that I described earlier. Donald Miller also talks about the "existential vacuum" that hits you in the head if you stop after you accomplish something and then choose to return to the "log" state instead of getting yourself into a new challenging adventure. And believe me, it's not a pleasant experience (#beentheredonethat). "We will not transform by thinking and dreaming. We will transform by doing" – something he recently posted on his Facebook page. I couldn't agree more. Logs don't transform and don't evolve (unless you're Pinocchio).

---

[62] Donald Miller, "Hero on a Mission: The Power of Finding Your Role in Life: The Path to a Meaningful Life" (2022)

You know how when you have something on your mind – you suddenly start seeing and hearing it everywhere: on the internet, on billboards, from your friends and colleagues? After reading "Hero on a Mission", I saw Andrew Huberman, the handsome PhD neuroscientist from Stanford I've been referencing in this book, talk about the same thing on Instagram. He just uses his own words but essentially he describes the same concept: "If you're spending your time and effort on something (anything), you would be wise to ensure the wins position you to face further meaningful challenges, not finish lines. Effort-win-effort-win... (infinitely repeated)... is the key."

In other words: **if you want to live a fulfilled happy life and avoid the "existential vacuum" – keep moving. But ensure that the activity you're engaged in is *enjoyable yet challenging*.**

I have to note here that this desperate search for a challenge to avoid "existential vacuum" is the burden (or a blessing? honestly, it's hard to say) of our society and our generation that has all their basic physical needs met. If you don't seem to be able to have your ends meet, then you're probably not worried about the meaning of life. With that said, you should still seek happiness, but there are other ways to do that, which are described in this book. But once you've covered the lower levels of needs from the Maslow pyramid – this is when the question "why am I even here?" starts bubbling up and keeps you up at night. Well, I hope that the version of the "meaning" described in this book helps you sleep better. It absolutely did the trick for me.

Another catchy quote from Donald Miller that I'd like to introduce to you: "Meaning happens when you've got a project that requires your unique abilities, an optimistic perspective on your challenges and when you have people to love. The 'people to love' part is my favorite."

Bonus: Live your life, don't just exist

This leads to another aspect of this discussion: the social component. **Social bonding – the process by which we form attachments – is vital for us as a species.**

Social bonding is not a specific behavior or a habit – it's a concept and it's essential for our happiness, that's why I'm squeezing it into this chapter. Humans are wired to form social bonds, it's not natural for us to be isolated. **We're unhappy when we're lonely.** Science explains[63] the neural and hormonal basis for "social homeostasis" – our drive for a given amount of socializing, which reveals why we get lonely and why we seek out connection with others. That's why COVID lockdowns had such a drastic effect on our overall happiness levels, worldwide.

What that means is that on top of everything we just learned together, one important thing we need to understand is: **meaningful connections with other humans matter, a lot** (10 extra points if you recognized another insight from the previous chapter). It doesn't mean you have to get out every night and force yourself to become a social butterfly if you're naturally an introvert (like me). What it means is that if you at least have a couple people in your life that you can share everything with – you're richer than Donald Trump.

So let's get "flowing"! And live our lives to the fullest and enjoy what we do. And love with open hearts. And be loved.

---

[63] Huberman Lab: Science of Social Bonding in Family, Friendship and Romantic Love (December 2021): https://hubermanlab.com/science-of-social-bonding-in-family-friendship-and-romantic-love/

● EXERCISE

DO THIS TODAY:

Google "36 questions to fall in love" (any website that the search returns – should do) and find a human in your closest circle that you're ready to open your heart to: it can be a friend, a loved one or someone you just would like to be closer to. Spend an evening answering these questions together. Read the instructions first. Once you're done, you'll be closer than ever. It's an amazing feeling that will make both of you happier. This exercise is also known to strengthen and deepen relationships between existing couples.

BTW, don't forget to have tissues handy.

DO THIS TODAY AND EVERY DAY, FOR THE REST OF YOUR LIFE:

Ask yourself "if I didn't have to work, what would I do in life"? Then go and do that.

Conclusion

Well, congrats! You're now fully equipped. You have no more excuses to not be happy.

If at this point you still feel some sort of attachment to your previous misery and feeling sorry for yourself instead of fully enjoying your life – that means there's some former trauma peaking out that you haven't yet dealt with. Reread the "Therapy and Psychedelics" chapter.

So let's summarize what we've learned.

First and foremost: **everything is in our heads.** It's the reactions to circumstances and our choices that shape our lives, it's not the circumstances themselves.

Second. **What you think about yourself is way more important than what others think about you.** How you feel about yourself shouldn't be dependent on what other people think about you. If you love YOU, you will be capable of truly loving others – not being addicted, not being dependent or possessive but truly loving, in a healthy way. So, if you want to live a high-quality life – be who you are. And accept it.

Full self-acceptance can lay the foundations for positive self-esteem, and the two frequently go hand-in-hand. Self-esteem stems from self-acceptance, which ultimately results in you being a much healthier (mentally healthier) human being.

As soon as you learn to accept yourself – you'll **stop judging others.** Learning to accept people for who they are, provides an incredible feeling of liberation that is almost as overwhelming as when you learn to accept yourself, which ultimately increases your happiness levels. Others will absolutely benefit if you stop trying to change them, but first of all, it will make YOU a happier person.

Then. **Don't be afraid to change your life.** Reorganize your routine in a way that **puts you at the top of your list of "important things in life".** Give yourself a chance to feel alive again: alive, respected and loved. You deserve it.

It's never too late to change. Most changes happen for the best and make us better, stronger and happier. Run periodic "retrospectives" of your life, do a cleanup, reorganize and optimize. Look back, reassess your life and make decisions to:

Stop – what makes you unhappy and adds stress (commitments, routines, jobs, relationships);

Continue – what is truly important, what strengthens your integrity, what makes you a better human in your own perception;

Start – new things that make you happier, more complete, that give you energy to evolve and become a better version of yourself, every day.

Clearly understanding what parts of your life make you happy and unhappy is half of the success and is a big step towards the new YOU. The second half of the success – is actually implementing it in your daily life.

Learn to **recognize your emotions and not be afraid of them.** First, there are no "bad" or "wrong" emotions. We have the right and the reason to feel what we feel at any point in time. Second, everything is temporary. EVERYTHING. Events, emotions, life itself. Again, it's all about perspective, which is entirely in our own heads. Recognize what you're feeling, label it, realize that there *will* be an end, face it, accept it, allow yourself to truly *feel*, and then see it leave your mind and body.

Remember that **being grateful for little things, and people, in your life** and actually training your brain to register those things is one of the most crucial elements of developing your new "happy" baseline.

Doing good things for others makes you happy, too. On top of that, it can also increase our feelings of social connection. Make sure to establish meaningful connections with others. **Social bonding is vital for us as a species.** Humans are wired to form social bonds, it's not natural for us to be isolated.

Important: **by no means should helping others come with a sacrifice to yourself.** This should *never* happen. Never do anything that would hurt you. Never sacrifice or allow others to take advantage of you.

Take care of your body. Emotions really capture the brain-body relationship. We cannot say that emotions arise just in our heads. They involve biological events in our bodies. So we want our bodies to be healthy in order to be able to process our emotions in a healthier way. There are three very important things that you can do to *help your body help you:* exercising regularly, sleeping well and eating healthy.

What's also important to understand: happiness lies not in the big things that we dream about, like a higher salary or a new house. It's in the little things that we miss if we're not paying attention. **Happiness lies in noticing little moments that give you joy.** The more you notice them, the more you register them, the more you remember them, the happier you are. Put down your phone. Be present. Learn to enjoy the little things.

Meditate. The positive effects of meditation have been proven again and again. Do it every day, for at least 10 minutes. You'll do yourself a huge favor and you'll move one step closer to becoming an ultimately serene and happy individual.

Experiences make you happier than "things". The activities you engage in should be ones that fit your values and interests, and that you actually enjoy.

What to aim for is the mental state in which you are fully immersed in a feeling of energized focus, full involvement, and enjoyment. This is the ultimate way of living a fulfilled, joyfull, happy life. Keep looking for those activities and you'll get there.

Meaning is in the movement. In other words, if you want to live a fulfilled happy life and avoid the "existential vacuum" – keep moving. But ensure that the activity you're engaged in is *enjoyable yet challenging.*

Live your life, don't just exist. Make a choice to only do things that you actually *love* doing rather than just living your life doing things you feel you *have* to do for whatever reason. It IS possible!

The above should help you with *understanding* the concepts of happiness. But as we discussed earlier, understanding and knowing is not enough. You need to actually practice it to teach your brain the skill of happiness.

Conclusion

So to get the most out of this book, try to make it a goal to practice all exercises outlined in each chapter. If this seems too overwhelming and you can't remember everything that you read – here's a short list of simple essential things you can start with:

- Make sure to get 7-8 hours of sleep every night and go to sleep at the same time

- In the morning, hug yourself and accept yourself for who you are

- Think about what makes you happy, allocate time to do it at least a couple times a week

- Do one nice thing for someone else on a daily basis

- Be present, as much as you can

- Perform physical activity at least 3 times a week for at least 30 minutes

- Avoid caffeine and alcohol (okay on occasion but not daily)

- Practice guided meditation every day at the same time for 10 minutes

- Before you go to bed every night, notice how you're feeling and write down 3 things you're grateful for today

Keep practicing and then reread this book again in a month. First of all, you'll be a whole new person by then. Second, you'll see more things and understand some of them on a deeper level than before. You'll be able to incorporate more tools into your routine and make them a natural part of your life.

I personally went through all the steps that I described in this book and practiced all of these tools. I'm still committed to all of them. They are a big, and a very natural, part of my life. They helped me survive physical abuse followed by a painful breakup, when my self esteem hit the floor and my entire existence was in question, when I had to figure out how to raise two little kids as a single mother while trying to rebuild my shattered identity, piece by piece.

These tools helped me go from being a ghost with one foot "on the other side" to one of the most energetic and eternally happy human beings you would ever meet, who is not afraid to feel, to live and to love. I didn't become a senseless robot or a helpless shadow despite all that I've been through, thanks to this knowledge and these tools in my arsenal. I am full of life and I am grateful for every single day and every single moment. I know how to live and how to love and I have a lot to give: to my kids, friends, loved ones, and to YOU personally.

As I said in the beginning, I wrote this book for YOU in the hope that you will take full advantage of this knowledge and turn your life in the direction of complete contentment and happiness that you can also share with others. You deserve to be happy. *You deserve to take care of yourself. You deserve to have an amazing life, full of excitement. Because you're awesome. I hope you know this.*

So get up, shrug, smile, and live a fulfilling, happy, and healthy life full of joy.

Thank you for committing to your happiness and reading this book. It truly means a lot to me.

Made in the USA
Las Vegas, NV
26 April 2024